This Changes Everything

Advance Praise for
This Changes Everything

"Long ago, I wrote a short note to Sonya Joy Mack with three words: 'Write that book.' And here it is! Sonya has penned a thoughtful, faith-filled story of hope and healing. This magical story will take you on an incredible journey that will keep you guessing until you reach the final pages."

-JENNIFER DUKES LEE, author of *Growing Slow* and *It's All Under Control*

"The fresh and funny voice of this new author is delightful. Sonya Joy Mack reveals her creativity in this unique and touching display of a mother/daughter's love for one another. Filled with light in the darkness and joy through the rain, this inspiring book will leave you with both laughter and tears. I give this debut novel five stars and five boxes of tissues!"

-ELAINE MARIE COOPER, author of *Sacred Vessels* and *Love's Kindling*

"Sonya Mack's book *This Changes Everything* is an affectionate and often humorous tale of a mother and daughter's travels and escapades. But even more, it is a fresh look at grief—how to hold loved ones close through the interweaving of our memories and imagination. An uplifting read for everyone."

-SUSAN R. LAWRENCE, author of *Restoration at River's Edge*, he *Blue Marble*, and T*he Long Ride Home*

"A daughter's tender tribute to the life and light of her beloved mother; a story that welcomes each of us to make the most of our moments and cherish our memories. Sonya Mack gracefully extends an invitation to see how goodness intermingles with grief—and how this simple shift in perspective changes everything."

-RACHEL MARIE KANG, author of *Let There Be Art*

"Sonya Joy Mack's debut work is proof that love transcends time and even death. Full of imagination and heart."

-**WYSTERIA EDWARDS, BA, EdM,** author of *Waiting for Mr. Rogers*

"*This Changes Everything* is a charmingly portrayed tale of love and loss. The author, Sonya Joy Mack, has beautifully and creatively depicted the bond between mother and daughter as they travel through the mountains and valleys of life. I connected with the author and what she went through on so many levels. The book will help you to see Sunshine on life's rainy days."

-**KATY PARKER,** wellbeing writer and blogger, Journeyofsmiley—Smile Through the Pain, Dance in the Rain

THIS CHANGES

Everything

WHEN DEATH NO LONGER
HAS THE FINAL SAY

SONYA JOY MACK

NEW YORK

LONDON • NASHVILLE • MELBOURNE • VANCOUVER

This Changes Everything

When Death No Longer Has the Final Say

Published in New York, New York, by Morgan James Publishing. Morgan James is a trademark of Morgan James, LLC. www.MorganJamesPublishing.com

Proudly distributed by Ingram Publisher Services.

Scripture quotations taken from The Holy Bible, New International Version® NIV® Copyright© 1973 1978 1984 2011 by Biblica, Inc.™ Used by permission. All rights reserved worldwide.

Morgan James BOGO™

A **FREE** ebook edition is available for you or a friend with the purchase of this print book.

CLEARLY SIGN YOUR NAME ABOVE

Instructions to claim your free ebook edition:
1. Visit MorganJamesBOGO.com
2. Sign your name CLEARLY in the space above
3. Complete the form and submit a photo of this entire page
4. You or your friend can download the ebook to your preferred device

ISBN 9781631959110 paperback
ISBN 9781631959127 ebook
Library of Congress Control Number: 2022933238

Cover Design by:
Rachel Lopez
www.r2cdesign.com

Interior Design by:
Christopher Kirk
www.GFSstudio.com

Morgan James PUBLISHING *with...* **Habitat for Humanity®** Peninsula and Greater Williamsburg

Builds

Morgan James is a proud partner of Habitat for Humanity Peninsula and Greater Williamsburg. Partners in building since 2006.

Get involved today! Visit MorganJamesPublishing.com/giving-back

To Joe,
the one who never gave up on me;
my forever companion on this journey.

To Mom,
the one who always believed in me;
I'll never forget you.

TABLE OF CONTENTS

Acknowledgments xi

The Beginning Of The End 1
Another One Of My Brothers 3
The Dead Leg 9
Live A Little Joy 15
Dancing Queen 19
Time To Enjoy The View 25
Life Is A Gift 31
The Heartbeat Of God 39
Wet Skivvies 45
Commando Style 49
The Secret 53
Never Again 57
A New Hope 61
Trust Me 67
Just Breathe 71
Redemption 77
Return Policy 83
Tori 87
The Mob 93

Let Your Hair Down 99

Embellishments. 105

The Past. 111

Glimpse Of Heaven. 117

Keep The Joy. 121

Something Is Wrong 123

Not My Plan 129

Whatever Is To Come 137

Pitocin. 141

The Arrival 147

Sweet Sophia 153

His Plan, Not Mine. 157

A Peace Worth Fighting For. 163

Disconnect 169

Brace For Impact. 173

The Verse. 177

The Results 181

An Unexpected Gift. 187

It's Time 191

It Is Done 195

Finally Home 201

Mountain Top. 207

The End Is The Beginning. 215

Alive In My Memories. 217

A Letter To My Mother. 223

Author's Note 227

Photo Gallery 228

About The Author. 231

ACKNOWLEDGMENTS

This book has been a five-year process from idea to the completed project you are reading now. There are so many people who have impacted me along the way I could write another book about all the people I want to thank. Still, since I'm only allowed a limited space, I will do my very best to include as many as possible.

I have to start by thanking God. He is the reason I am here and the actual author of this story. He weaved so many people into my life to help along the way. May all the glory truly go to Him.

To the entire team at Morgan James Publishing (Terry, Cortney, Heidi, Emily, Jim, David, the design and author relations team members, and everyone else I forgot to mention here), how could I possibly express my gratitude? You took a risk on an unknown author, a small-town Iowa girl with a big dream and a story on her heart. You all have been incredible from the initial introduction to the final release.

Word Weavers and Sharpened Pencils family, especially Elaine, Judy, Sherry, Diane, Glenda, my editor Angela Johnson, and my proofreader Amy Myers: you have all been instrumental in helping a young writer learn how to become an author. Thank you for your endless support and encouragement.

To the doctors, nurses, and staff at MercyOne Des Moines hospital, NICU, and OR. Thank you for being the real heroes in such a huge part of this story. You helped my family and me through a challenging time, and I will forever be grateful. Thank you for saving my children's lives. And to Dr. Lampe and the entire Kossuth County Hospice team, thank you for the kindness and love you poured out to my family at a very difficult time.

To my Soul Sisters and my true believers (Lindsey, Brenda, Christine, Keara, Rachel, Wystie, Barb B., and so many more) for never doubting I could do it. Thank you for always asking how the book was going, even when the answer was, "it's coming," for almost three years.

I have to thank my LIVE JOY LIFE family for trusting me in your inbox and allowing me to share my words and heart with you.

For my family: Aunt Tina and Uncle Rich, Dad, Shane, and Wendy, thank you for being a part of my life, helping me keep the memories of Mom alive, and for answering my late-night texts and phone calls when I missed her so much.

To my incredible husband Joe and my babies, Lillian and Sophia, this book is your story as much as it is mine. Your constant support, encouragement, and unwavering belief in me are far more valuable than I could ever explain. You, my true loves, have changed everything.

To Mom. I miss you every single day. I will never forget that no one loved me as you did. Save a place for me.

"THIS CHANGES EVERYTHING,"
is based on a true story.
Some names have been changed to protect privacy."

THE BEGINNING OF THE END

Whish, whoosh, hum. Whish, whoosh, hum.

The oxygen concentrator hummed in time with the ventilator's mechanical breath—their sounds a heavy reminder of the life they afforded in the next room. For two years, their rhythms filled my childhood home.

There was no need for the alarm I'd set. Sleep had evaded me most of the night. Sneaking out of bed, careful not to wake my husband, I crept up the stairs, needing one last moment with her before the others arrived. The coolness of the laminate kitchen floor jolted my already heightened senses. Even the warmth of the carpet as I crossed into the living room couldn't soothe me today. Now cluttered with medical equipment, the once ample area resembled a hospital room rather than a family gathering space. The medicinal smell burned my nose.

Echoing her place in our family, Mom lay in the center of the room, sleeping peacefully on her hospital bed, thanks to a morphine drip. Her muted, pale skin hung loosely over her atrophied muscles. The image forever imprinted in my mind.

Fighting back the tears, I approached her quietly as the gravity of what was coming fused with my soul. Slipping my cool fingers into her warm hand, I extended a small squeeze, one she could no longer return. Her eyelids fluttered open as the faintest smile parted her lips.

"Good morning, Sunshine," her voice, muffled and slurred by disease, was challenging to understand.

"Good morning, beautiful." My own words caught on the pain in my throat. "Can I lay with you for a bit?"

Her eyes had already closed, weighed down by the pull of the morphine. Lowering the bed rail, I snuggled into her. Placing her arm over my chest, I lay next to the woman who had been my whole world, my best friend for twenty-nine years, and the reality of the day cracked my resolve. Tears I'd fought to contain landed in silent stains on her bedsheets.

Snuggling into her warmth, I drifted into a memory. I was nine years old, curled up on my mother's lap, my head resting on her chest, the way I often did. Inhaling her sweet perfume that always reminded me of home, I pressed my ear against her and listened to the soft *lub-dub* of her heart as it pumped steadily.

It was there, nestled in her protective arms, I would imagine our future together. Even as a child, I knew she was more than my mother. She was my compass, the one thing that always led me back home. Lulled by the beat of her heart, I would envision her next to me when my children were born and picture a day we could embark on adventures our modest lifestyle couldn't afford.

"Where should we go today, Mom? You want mountains, ocean, or maybe Disney?"

"You choose today, Sunshine. Just don't forget the fun." Her voice was barely audible, weakened by her tired, diseased body.

Leaning my head onto her, I whispered, "Okay, Mom, I'll take you everywhere."

We lay together in silence as I tried to soak up every bit of her memory before the remainder of my family began to wake.

ANOTHER ONE OF MY BROTHERS

My five-foot two-inch mother gazed in apprehension at the giant horse she intended to mount, and only one thought crossed my mind—this was going to be good.

Rising over the great Rocky Mountains, the sun mirrored light off snow-tipped peaks. Typical for early June in Colorado, the cool morning breeze tickled my skin. Tiny goosebumps traveled up my arms—a sensation I knew well. I was always cold. My internal temperature had never readjusted from years spent in frigid lecture halls and science labs. Even from a young age, the ebb and flow of the body's internal rhythm filled me with awe.

I had applied myself through six years of relentless academia. I shuddered at the memory. School was my full-time job and, though I was good at it, the demand left little in the way of time or money for the travels I'd longed for in my youth.

My childhood wasn't glamorous, but it was reliable. It was nothing like the tumultuous nature of her childhood. For that, I was forever grateful. Looking at her now, I wondered if she would someday tell me about the childhood she kept so secret.

As children, we weren't raised to go to church every week, memorize Bible verses, or say prayers gathered around the table. Still, my mother spoke reverently of God and Jesus. It was a faith she shared only with those closest to her, as if faith and loving Jesus was something she wasn't doing well enough. She was more comfortable sharing her deep faith modestly with those dearest to her through her generosity or kindness. I shared my mother's quiet faith, afraid my lack of knowledge would somehow render me inadequate.

Jerked from thought as Chuck, the sweet old gelding I sat on, shifted his weight under me, I caught my breath before feeling his mane tickle my hand as it flowed in the wind.

"Hey there, old boy." I patted his thinning coat, scattering dust into the sunlight. He huffed a breath of hot air onto my leg.

Deciding to start our mother-daughter vacation on a horseback ride through the mountains, I'd managed to find my way quickly into my saddle. Despite my time lost in thought, I noticed Mom still stood in front of hers. Though she appeared to be in deep discussion with Hugo, our tour guide, I was confident she had no idea what he was saying. With high-pitched giggles and sideways glances, she'd ogled him since our arrival. Hugo's rolled-up flannel shirt-sleeves revealed his dark tan, and his tight jeans had her grinning like a schoolgirl.

"Just another one of my brothers," she'd whispered into my ear as we strode toward him earlier.

"Mother, you know I think that's the weirdest phrase. Why do you say that when you think someone's attractive?"

"Because I'm a married woman." She placed her hand on her heart, a gesture of fidelity. "So, if I say he's my brother, that means we share the same genes, *and* I'm not hitting on another man." Her tone was serious, as if her rationalization made perfect sense.

Standing next to him now, I could see her admiration hadn't changed. She could hardly contain herself when Hugo offered her a hand to mount her horse. Steadying her foot in the stirrup, she looked up apprehensively at the distance to her saddle. I closed one eye, afraid to watch. With a swift movement, Hugo's help, and an act of God's grace, she landed upright and forward on her seat. Finally, atop the horse, she waved back at me.

Her round face was dusted with freckles and a grin that had settled into her cheeks with age. I shook my head, returning her wave, surprised a middle-aged woman could be so adorable. As she wiggled her booty in the saddle, likely adjusting her seating, I placed a gentle heel into Chuck's side and motioned for him to move forward. He plodded slowly, positioning me closer to Mom.

"Just like the old saddle show days?" I grinned mischievously. Growing up on a farm with a small arena in the front pasture, she often participated in her family's local horse shows.

Her gaze was fixed off in the distance as if she were somewhere else entirely. It was moments before she shuddered, turning back to me. "Goodness. That was a long time ago. I'm pretty sure the reason I made it up here was more a miracle and less about previous experience."

Her last few words faded out as she let out a quick grunt. "And now I can't seem to get my darn foot in this stirrup." She stared at her leg as if willing it to reach the stirrup that hung about three inches too low.

"Mom," I laughed despite my best efforts. "I don't think you can will your leg to grow. Why don't you ask Hugo to adjust the strap?"

She lowered her voice. "I've already asked Hugo to adjust it twice, and I don't want to bother him again. I'm pretty sure he thinks I have an old lady crush on him. It'll be fine once we get going." Despite her slight inconvenience, she was always the optimist and was determined to have a delightful time. She never ceased to be a source of laughter, usually unwittingly.

A little concerned she'd regret her decision, I suggested she ask Hugo to fix the stirrup once more.

"I'm not worried." She dismissed my comment with a wave. "I'm sure it'll be fine."

"Alright. But, I don't want to hear any complaining later." Reaching for my reins, I guided Chuck toward Hugo's mare.

"Okay. Let's go." She turned her face forward into the sun, and happiness beamed from her smile, a feeling I couldn't help but mirror as I allowed myself to relax in a way I hadn't for years.

Hugo's brown eyes scanned the crowd, ensuring everyone was seated. Pleased with what he saw, he began a brief riding lesson, his thick Southern drawl accentuating each command. When I looked over at Mom, she still seemed more interested in looking at Hugo than listening to him.

I leaned toward her. "You should probably pay better attention to what Hugo is saying."

Her eyes darted in my direction. "I am listening."

"Uh-huh. Sure you are." I winked.

She placed a pink polished finger to her lips. "Shh, you're interrupting." Then, flicking her hand to indicate that was enough, we both turned back to our instructor.

After his tutorial, Hugo placed us all in a single file line. We began our slow climb up the mountain with Chuck and I second to Hugo's mare and Mom following behind us. The ride was scheduled for two hours, and I was anxious to take it all in, having never seen mountains before.

Not more than thirty minutes into the ride, it became clear our sightseeing adventure would be more entertainment than awe.

To my mother's unfortunate luck, Chuck had a bit of a flatulence problem. Every few minutes, I heard her spit and sputter behind me, "Blugh, yuck."

"You okay back there?" I turned around to see what the fuss was.

She fanned her face. "Oh, it's nothing. Your horse just has a little gas."

"Oh, shoot." I smiled slightly. Being upwind, I wasn't affected by any odor. Still, I could imagine how the cover of evergreen trees we were traveling through might intensify Chuck's musk. The thought made me giggle. "I'm really sorry. Anything I can do?"

"No. I'll just keep fanning myself as we go." She waved her hand feverishly in front of her face.

"Are you sure? I can ask Hugo to put me in back." I pointed to the end of the line of horses with riders.

"Absolutely not. I'm not going to let a little gas spoil your view from the front."

It was like her to put our needs before her own, and the recollection comforted me.

Despite Chuck's unfortunate case of intestinal distress, we proceeded up the mountain. The jingle of the bridle and clop of the horseshoes against the rocky trail provided the perfect accompaniment to our ride. Though the endless rolling hills of Iowa were beautiful in their own way, the slated mountains with evergreens dotting their sides were beyond what my heart could comprehend.

Turning in my saddle, I recognized the sparkle of awe in Mom's eyes. Her free hand rested, palm down, on her chest. I could almost feel the joy pulsing through her.

When we reached the summit of our journey, Hugo stopped so the group could look out over the landscape. Our horses, well trained after years on the trail, turned instinctively toward the valley. Purple columbine offset by golden blanket flowers created a backdrop that surpassed my imagination. Butterflies, shimmering in the sunlight, speckled their surface. A distant deer stood with its white tail erect.

"Look, Sonya." Her voice was soft, almost reverent. "Isn't it beautiful? Look at those butterflies. Such beautiful creatures that fly free without a care in the world." Witnessing their delicate wings and vibrant colors, weightless in the sky, caught me off guard, and I felt the prick of tears in my eyes.

"What's the matter, Sunshine?"

I turned back toward the outlook. "Nothing, Mom. I'm just so happy to be spending this time with you. It makes me feel whole again."

Despite being separated by our equestrian friends, she stretched for my hand. Barely able to reach, we locked little fingers. Hers, as always, was warm compared to mine—a welcome reminder of her sincere soul.

"Sunshine." My nickname struck a heart chord I hadn't expected. As a child, she would lull me to sleep singing "You Are My Sunshine" as she ran her fingers through my auburn hair. "My little ray of sunshine," she'd whisper. The endearment stuck.

She turned toward me, her eyes locking with mine. "You don't ever have to live without me. A mother-daughter bond—that's a bond forged by God, and that bond can never be broken." Despite her reassurance, doubt still grappled at my heart.

We sat that way, fingers locked, lost in the portrait before us as I cherished the quiet moment we spent together.

After a few minutes of treasured silence, Hugo announced it was time to head back. Turning toward the trail, our horses began down the mountainous terrain as I noticed Mom's generous smile. A lifetime of love etched in her features. How blessed I was that God chose her to be my mother.

THE DEAD LEG

"A hh. Oomph. Ugh." Lulled by the rustle of pine needles and the sun's warmth on my skin as we descended the trail, I vaguely heard the guttural noises behind me.

"Psst. Sonya."

As we neared the barn, Mom's voice, and the distraction, grew louder.

"Sonya."

Sensing the urgency in her voice, I twisted in my saddle to face her. "What's going on? And why are you whisper-shouting?"

She gaped at me, face contorted in confusion. "What's whisper-shouting? That doesn't make sense." Taking only a moment to process my statement, she waved it off. "Oh, never mind. I need your help."

"With what?" I recognized the concern on her face.

"Well . . ." she started, looking away in embarrassment. "I think I should have had Hugo fix the stirrup because now I can't feel my leg." She continued in a hushed tone, probably realizing Hugo was a mere horse length ahead of me.

"What do you mean you can't 'feel your leg?'" I tossed in some air quotes as I furrowed my brow. Given her propensity toward quirkiness, I was used to her not making sense.

"Just what I said. I can't feel my leg! It fell asleep on the ride because I didn't have anything to rest it on." Her eyes darted about as if searching for the answer. "How the heck am I gonna get off this horse?"

"Calm down, Mom." I held up my hand and fought back the urge to laugh. "Move your foot back and forth to get some blood flowing into it. I'm sure once we stop, Hugo can help you down." Though I tried to reassure her, the look on her face revealed it wasn't working.

"I don't even think Hugo can help!" Real panic had set in. Her voice neared hysterics

On cue to test our theory, we arrived at the barn. Hugo's deep voice instructed us to steer our horses toward the fence, dismount if we could, and hand the reins to one of the workers standing by. The long ride had made my muscles stiff, but I swung my leg over Chuck's back and landed on the dirt below with surprising ease. Feet to the ground, I looked over at Mom. Still seated on top of her horse, she furiously rubbed her leg.

"How's it going?" I asked after making my way to her side.

"Not so well. There is no way I'm getting off of here. They're going to have to call in a crane. This leg is dead." She gave her leg a good, hard slap.

Hoping to calm her panic, I rested my hand on her arm. "Don't worry. Everything's going to be fine. I'll go get Hugo and see what he can do."

Before she could protest, I jogged over to our handsome tour guide. "Excuse me, sir." He turned toward me, revealing his dark chocolate eyes. Taken aback by his rugged good looks, I caught myself staring. Feeling the heat of embarrassment spread across my cheeks, I blinked twice to clear my head. "Sorry to bother you, Sir, but I think my mom's going to need a little assistance getting off her horse." I caught a laugh before it could escape, then pointed in Mom's direction. She flashed an embarrassed smile, and half waved in our direction with all eyes on her.

Hugo uttered a simple, "Happy to help," then tipped his hat as his mouth pulled into a tight smile. Turning quickly, he jogged over to where Mom sat alone, still in her saddle.

Not wanting to miss any action, I followed.

"What seems to be the matter, Ma'am?" Hugo asked, wiping a bit of sweat from his brow.

She explained about the stirrup being too low and how she was sorry she didn't ask him to fix it again. As she spoke, I watched her pale face blush crimson.

"Don't worry, Ma'am. I'll help you get down. This sort of thing happens all the time." He walked to the side of the barn and pulled a generous-sized plywood box over to her horse.

Though it was tempting to stand by and enjoy the show, I decided to see if there was any way I could help.

Even from behind them, I could hear Hugo's voice, soft and reassuring with a quiet Southern drawl. "Okay, Ma'am. I'm gonna stand over here on this box. Then, I'll ask your daughter to help you swing your dead leg over the horse." He fought against the grin that pulled at his lips as he uttered the word 'dead.' Without missing a beat, he continued his directions. "What I need from you is to keep your good leg in the stirrup, so you have something to bear your weight. I'll catch you over here on this box." He stomped his boot to the plywood kicking up a mist of dust. "Understand?"

If Mom's face was any indication, she wasn't sure the plan was going to work. Not willing to accept the alternative, she nodded in agreement. "I'll do whatever you say."

"Don't worry, Mom. We've got this." I snorted.

"Sonya Joy!" Though the exclamation of my middle name usually meant I was in trouble, the friendly look on her face exposed her scolding as more nervousness than a warning.

"Don't worry," I repeated. "Just make sure your good foot is in that stirrup." Pointing to the worn brown loop on which her foot was perched, I continued. "Or you'll end up on the floor."

Sensing her hesitancy, Hugo piped up. "Just like I said, ma'am, this happens all the time."

I appreciated his gesture to reassure her, but if the nervous energy force field surrounding us were any indication, this would not end well. "Now, does everyone know what they're going to do?"

Mom and I locked stares. With a quick nod of her head, she straightened her body and adjusted herself in her saddle.

"Okay then," his voice as sturdy as his physique, "on the count of three. One. Two. Three."

On 'three,' I heaved her dead leg as hard as I could over the saddle. Likely focused on Hugo's reminder to keep her good foot in the stirrup, Mom neglected to hold onto anything with her hands. Her leg catapulted toward Hugo, followed quickly by her entire body.

In his panic to keep her off the ground, one of Hugo's hands landed directly on Mom's bottom. Caught off guard on her way down, she toppled into him. In Hugo's struggle to keep her upright as Mom teetered near the edge, he grabbed whatever he could—Mom's bosom.

Shocked by her sudden circumstance, Mom screeched, "Oh, my!"

Hugo's humiliation was instant. He quickly moved his hand to her shoulder, steadying her frame. "I'm so sorry, Ma'am! I didn't mean to be inappropriate. I was just tryin' to keep you from fallin' to the ground." A slight cherry glow flushed his chestnut skin.

"Oh goodness, of course, you didn't mean it. Why would a handsome young man like you try to grope an old lady like me?"

"Mom!" I blurted. She was always naive to her lack of verbal filter, and my mortification bubbled. I covered my eyes, attempting to hide from the awkwardness. Though her naivety was endearing, it bordered on ridiculous.

"What? He is good-looking. And I know he was just trying to help."

"Mom! Seriously, *stop talking*." I shouted under my breath.

"What did I say?" Her confusion was genuine.

Hugo was traumatized. He stared, wide-eyed at his hands, and flipped them back and forth, as if in disbelief of what had just taken place. Trying to put the poor man out of his misery, I graciously thanked him and grabbed Mom's hand.

I whipped around and whispered into her ear. "Thank the poor man, and let's get going."

Still holding her hand, I drug her along. We'd taken quite a few steps before I realized she was having trouble keeping up. "Why are you walking like that?" I asked. With each step, she limped with her legs spread wide open.

"I told you, my leg is still dead, and I feel like my crotch is stuck in this position." She waved her hands quickly, indicating her nether region. "Give me a second, and I'm sure they'll wake up."

My laughter exploded. Tears streamed from my eyes as my abdomen spasmed. Doubled over, unable to speak, I allowed the waves to continue for nearly a minute as Mom gawked from the side, hands on her hips in mock frustration. As my convulsions began to subside, I stood up, catching my breath.

"You done yet?" She swirled her finger in my direction.

I inhaled sharply, abating any remaining laughter. "Yeah, I'm finished." I ran my fingers through my hair before exhaling sharply. "Let's get back in the car. I think we've had enough fun for one day."

As I offered her my hand, a deep dimple pierced the center of her cheek as it always did when she smiled from her most genuine place. She hooked her arm in mine as we continued our slow pace back to the car. In the aftermath of the moment, feeling her warmth next to me, gratitude melded into my heart.

August 2011

LIVE A LITTLE JOY

Growing up, our family home was a modest ranch on the outskirts of a small town in Iowa. Now that I was an adult, it was there that I sat cross-legged on the couch, with mom in the chair across from me, reminiscing over some of our favorite memories. It was a past time I loved as I grew into adulthood. Mid-sentence into my story, Mom laughed with such force, the coffee she'd sipped shot straight out of her mouth. The liquid carried impressive momentum, splattering against my cheek a few feet away.

"Mom!" I wiped the droplets from my face, shaking my head.

I should have been accustomed to her whimsical nature, but the unexpected display still caught me off guard. "What in the world is so funny you had to shower me in coffee?"

"Oh, I'm so sorry." Still half choking on her drink, she put a hand to her neck to catch her breath. "I just happen to remember that one time, when what's his name . . ." she snapped her fingers, as usual, attempting to recall the details. "Oh, you know. He had to help me because of my leg. Goodness, that was funny."

Notorious for phrasing sentences without using actual descriptors, statements like "what's her name" or "that one thing" frequented our conversations. Over the years, it had developed into an unwritten code only I could decipher.

"I'm assuming by 'what's his name' you mean Hugo, and by 'that one time' you mean when he had to help you off your horse because of your dead leg. Of course, I remember. It still goes down in my book as one of the funniest, most embarrassing moments of my life."

She swished her hand to dismiss my comment. "It wasn't that embarrassing."

"Yes, it was. You nearly took the poor guy out. If he hadn't caught you, you'd have ended up with a face full of dirt. In my book, that's embarrassing. But either way, what made you think of that?"

She shrugged. "Not sure. Just reminiscing, I suppose."

We often reflected on our trip to Colorado, especially the horseback ride that left Mom accidentally groped by a stable guy named Hugo.

During a rather short visit home that summer, our conversation centered around what our next excursion might be. A child at heart, she longed for a destination like Walt Disney World. At the same time, I suggested more adult locations such as Las Vegas or Mexico. However, the thought of my sweet, naive mother in the sinful whirlwind of Las Vegas made me laugh out loud.

"What would you do in Walt Disney World anyway?" I asked.

"To visit the princesses and Mickey, of course." A sheepish grin spread across her face.

"Mother, you're such a kid."

"Well, you," she waved an accusatory finger in my direction, "shouldn't take yourself so seriously. The world will bring you enough to be serious about. It's important to take advantage of the moments when you can live a little joy."

"Live a little joy, huh? Easier said than done, wouldn't you say?" All too often, I allowed the fear of embarrassment to hinder my joy. Mom, on the other hand, wore hers like a badge of honor.

When she looked at me, I caught the faintest hint of sadness in her eyes. "Sunshine, joy is easy. It's always accessible in your heart," she tapped her chest. "And right here," smiling as she indicated her mind. "The world might try to bring you down. But if there is one thing I have realized lately, it's that joy is woven into the very fiber of our beings. We're just in charge of letting it free."

I allowed her words to settle into my mind like the soil after a rainstorm filling in the crevasses. Still, the idea of joy being so easily accessible seemed unrealistic given everything I'd been through in recent years.

"That's a great thought, Mom, but it doesn't always seem that easy. What about when we're facing the hard stuff like grief, heartbreak, suffering, or any number of other emotions that don't feel very joyful?" I folded my arms across my chest, waiting for her reply.

"Sunshine, that's where faith comes in." She glanced upward as she rested her head against the back of the chair. "I've been doing a lot of talking with Jesus lately. Every day He reminds me that faith is a choice. We can choose faith amid all the bad stuff and know that hard times are part of growth. You know it takes a lot of time and patience to make a diamond, but it's absolutely beautiful once it's formed."

Though surprised by her sudden insight, I supposed she was right. I had witnessed her choose faith amid unbearable suffering and use it to shine a light of joy to those around her. I watched her faith radiate in moments of anguish. The weight of anguish that would have crushed me.

"You're probably right, Mom. Maybe I need to spend more time with Jesus, too." I winked.

"Definitely." Endearment settled onto her smile. "He's such a gentleman. He loves when you spend time with him." Her eyes met mine with every bit of seriousness in their depths.

"Sounds like you've gotten to know him pretty well." My mouth pulled into an intentional smile.

"I guess you could say that." A ray of sunshine broke through the clouds that previously lingered in the sky. The beam crossed the sliding door to the patio and landed near her face. Closing her eyes, she relaxed into the light.

Leaving my seat on the sofa, I went to her. Crawling my long body up onto the chair, I snuggled myself into her lap. It was ridiculous, really. I was almost thirty years old and at least six inches taller than her. It wasn't easy to scrunch myself up into a ball small enough to fit there anymore, but there was something about her holding me that made the world feel right again.

Resting my head on her chest as I often had when I was young. I focused on the soft "whish" of air as she inhaled and exhaled, her lungs easily expanding under my weight. Listening to her steady, reliable breath, I wondered how often I took something as simple, yet as vital as breathing for granted. The soft cadence of sounds filled me with a sense of safety. Outside the window, I noticed the petite butterfly fluttering near the glass.

"I miss you, Mom. Maybe you should just stay here with me." My voice muffled in her shoulder.

"Oh, Sunshine, I wish that's how it worked. For now, we can cherish the time we do spend together."

Our bond had morphed, in recent years, to one uniquely spiritual, and I savored every moment. I closed my eyes in gratitude as I nestled in further, concentrating on the soft rhythm of her breath.

May 2012

DANCING QUEEN

Des Moines had been my home for nearly six years, and I'd fallen in love with its big-city amenities and small-town charm. Growing up in a more modest farming community, I appreciated the culture and experience of my new urban home. Despite my love for my new hometown, long hours under my new professional title of Physician Assistant had left me exhausted—mentally and physically. The stress had begun to take its toll, and I'd invited Mom for a visit.

"Where are you?" It was a Friday afternoon, and I was incapable of being patient.

"I'm just about to pull onto your street." Her excitement, reflecting mine, reverberated through the phone.

"Wow! You are close. I'm so excited. It's been too long." Returning my phone to my pocket, I noticed Joe's smile from across the room. Mom's outward and loving personality gained her fast friends, and my husband was no exception.

"Your mom almost here?" He crossed the room and encircled me into a generous hug.

"Yes, and I can't wait. I've missed her." Feeling his strength around me, I relaxed into the years of comfort and protection they embodied.

"I'm glad you're spending some time together," he whispered, his breath releasing in hot puffs against my cheek. I closed my eyes, allowing his love to fill in all my empty places. Only he understood the true importance of Mom's visit.

I heard a car door shut outside. Beyond the window, I watched as her short frame emerged. One look at her dimple-dented cheeks, and I couldn't help but go to her.

I planted a quick kiss on Joe's cheek then swung the door open into the glaring sun.

"You're here!" I engulfed her into a tight embrace. She smelled of vanilla and honey, a scent reminiscent of home. I snuggled deeper into her shoulder. Her warmness radiated outward, a pleasant barrier against the cool spring breeze. We sustained our hug as if we could draw all the time between our meetings back into this moment.

"I've missed you," I whispered, so much weight carried on my words. Too much time had passed, and a pang of sadness touched my heart.

"I missed you too, Sunshine. You haven't asked me to visit much this year. But I know you've been busy." She placed her delicate hands on the sides of my cheeks, bringing my face closer to hers. Her eyes pierced through mine. She'd witnessed my hardships and toils, even from afar, and I recognized her unspoken acknowledgment. "But I'm here now, so let's make the most of it."

My stomach groaned audibly.

"Sounds like somebody's hungry." She poked me playfully in the softest part of my belly.

"Yeah. I didn't get a chance to eat much today. The Urgent Care was slammed, and I hate making patients wait while I eat—even if it's only ten minutes."

Wrinkles furrowed between her brows. I knew the look well. She was always worried about her kids, our safety and security protected like a precious jewel. She always said her children were her life.

"Sonya Joy." Her voice lowered.

I raised a finger to stop her from commenting further. "I know, Mom. Can we talk about it over dinner? I'm starving."

"Alright, but you need to take better care of yourself." She dusted a stray hair from my cheek.

*****

Friday night in the big city meant most restaurants would be overflowing with hungry families and business types winding down after a long week. I picked one close to a shopping district. If we'd have to wait long, at least we could use our time wisely.

My suspicions were confirmed when we reached the establishment. Inside was a flurry of patrons, hungry and eager to take their seats. The reverberation of voices came across the large space at an alarming volume, while the smell of peanuts, freely discarded on the floor, filled the room. We scooted our way to the hostess, apologizing as we knocked elbows with the crowds of people waiting for tables.

"The wait's about ninety minutes." The twenty-something blonde behind the counter announced before writing our name on the list.

"Thanks." I shifted toward Mom. Her eyes darted quickly about the scene as she took it all in. The bar bustled with you adults and people in suits reveling at the start of their weekend. I tapped her shoulder, catching her attention. "Busy in here, isn't it? Want to go check out a store or two while we wait?"

"Please!" She would never turn down an invitation to shop.

Not wanting to lose our spot in line, we decided to stick to the clothing store nearest the restaurant. It was one of my favorites, but the music inside often blared at deafening levels. With conversation difficult, we began to meander throughout the store. Distracted by racks of trendy clothes and the beat of the music, less than five minutes later, I realized I could no longer see her.

"Where did she go?" I mumbled. Though the store was only average in size, it was divided into three separate spaces with multiple dressing rooms anchoring each side—plenty of places for her to hide. My eyes scanned the aisles, searching each separate area before finally locating her near the back of the store, barely visible over the racks.

One look at her, and an instant blush flushed my face. Her small figure bounced as her even shorter arms fist-pumped the air to the music like a charged teenager. I was mortified.

"Mom!" I shouted above the music, hesitant to get close, fearing someone might suspect this dancer was with me.

"Do you have to dance like that? It's embarrassing."

"What?" she yelled back.

I moved slightly closer, closing the gap between us.

"What? I can't hear you." She pointed to her ear.

I inched further in her direction, attempting to hide from view. "I said, your dancing is embarrassing."

"I can't help it," her voice still yelling. "It's so catchy. You should try it."

"Mother! Seriously. Do I have to take you back home?" Her child-like personality occasionally resulted in my chagrin, though more my fault than hers. I was never sure why I always put so much pressure on myself to be perfect and put together—living like I had something to prove. While I should have followed her lead to loosen up and enjoy life, instead, I found myself embarrassed and uncomfortable.

She noticed the look on my face, her own expression sympathetic. "If it bothers you that much, I'll stop, but you should lighten up. Learn to live a little. Find some joy, remember?" Lightly pinching my cheek, her spirited laugh sprung out over the music.

Secretly, seeing her dance, arms and legs moving freely to the beat was a welcome sight. I wished I could share her light-hearted attitude, but my type-A personality usually left me devoid of her free spirit. Though I had to admit, her playfulness was contagious. I turned my head so she couldn't witness the smile that drew across my face.

*****

The remainder of the weekend was perfect. We shared old family stories over a cheese flight and dessert at my favorite French restaurant. We enjoyed the upscale, eclectic shops of the East Village. With a visit to my favorite winery, we anticipated future endeavors over Pinot Noir while we both danced to the music. As Sunday night neared, so did my sadness.

We stood in the driveway, the sun beginning to duck below the horizon. For a moment, I stared into the watercolor rays that jetted from its center. I longed to stay there, in the space between memory and reality.

"I had so much fun with you this weekend." My head found its familiar space near her neck as I wrapped my arms around her. Her sweet scent filled me.

"I had the best time too, Sunshine."

As with most times we parted ways, tears pricked at my eyes before overflowing onto my cheeks. Though I was a grown, capable woman, something about the comfort of my mother's presence soothed all of life's open wounds.

Hugging her tighter, I tried to collect the love she possessed and secure it inside until the next time. "We can talk every day, right?"

"Of course, we can. I'm always here to listen."

"It's just not the same as seeing you," my words barely audible.

"I know. But we will be together again soon."

We may be together again, but it would feel like a lifetime. I clutched her one last time and whispered, "I miss you."

"I miss you too, Sunshine."

Though I tried to fight the tears, I knew I was failing. I opened her car door and offered a hand as she stepped in. Her smile was angelic in the final light of the setting sun. With one last kiss to her forehead, I gently closed the door.

The rocks crunched beneath her tires as she backed out of the drive. Making a sharp turn onto the road, I noticed her reflection through the tinted glass. Her mouth was pulled into a familiar smile as she waved feverishly in my direction. My heart squeezed with reminiscent grief as I watched her car disappear into the darkening night.

My emotions threatened to betray my fortitude. Wetness continued down my cheeks. Wiping it away, I waved once more into the blackness her absence left. "See you again soon."

My feet shuffled toward the house as I whispered a silent, grateful prayer.

October 2012

TIME TO ENJOY THE VIEW

They say silence is deafening, which I might agree, when weighed down by the burden of a secret. I sat motionless in my seat, the hum of the plane a welcome companion to my thoughts. Each breath deliberate against the force of the secret I held. I knew I would tell her eventually, but now wasn't the time. After all, I was still unsure of how I felt about the news. Both fear and excitement pulsed through my veins, with neither yet the true winner. Shaking the thought from my head, I glanced over at Mom, hoping she hadn't noticed my distraction.

On the edge of her seat, her face pressed against the airplane window, she bounced like an excited Chihuahua waiting for a treat. Taking her in, I nearly choked on the final drops of water I'd just sipped.

"Ladies and Gentlemen, we have started our initial descent into Orlando. Please return to your seats and ensure your seatbelts are fastened. It's been a pleasure having you fly with us today." The captain's voice blared over the speakers, startling Mom. "Flight attendants, please prepare for landing."

Still new to the flying experience, she ceased bouncing and steadied herself at the captain's announcement. I sensed her fingers as they reached for mine. The ironic nature of our story never ceased to delight me. My mom was fiercely protective, yet her lack of big-world experiences often left me in a more parental role. Her hand pinched mine as she gripped it with the plane's descent.

"Oh, I still don't like this part," her voice quivered.

"It's okay, Mom. It helps if you remember you're more likely to die in a car accident than a plane crash." I smirked.

"Sonya Joy! Don't say that. Crashing is the *futherest* thing from my mind."

"Speaking Vicklish again?" Family banter pressed my mouth into a wide grin.

"What did I say wrong this time?" She huffed, frustrated.

Our family's running joke was that my mother spoke her own language. With a combination of her name, Vicki, and her native language, English, we referred to her spoken dialect as "Vicklish." Though we enjoyed the quip quite frequently, her quick look of annoyance made it clear she wasn't equally amused.

"Futh-er-est is not a word. I think you meant farthest. What you meant to say was 'Crashing to your death in an airplane was the *farthest* thing from your mind.'" I grinned mischievously.

"You better watch it, young lady, or you're going to get it." A stubby finger waved in my direction, though her smile betrayed her warning.

"Get it, huh? You've been saying I'm going to 'get it' for years, but I never have."

Opening my mouth to reply, she stopped me. "Oh, hush. Just hold my hand and stop picking on me until we land."

"But it's so much fun." I took her hand, surrounding it with my own, and noticed the freckles that dusted her skin. *At least that hasn't changed.* Running my thumb along her skin, I hoped the sentiment would relay even an ounce of the grace she'd shown me over the years. She'd always been an easy target for our wisecracks, and I hoped she didn't harbor any real embarrassment. Glancing up, I could see the features of her face begin to relax, haloed by the sunlight.

Her figure, though small, housed so much of what I strived to be—a deep, passionate love for family and God, simplistic gratitude for life, and unparalleled generosity. I squeezed her hand, hoping to convey my gratitude.

"You okay over there?" I was nervous that my comment really had hurt her feelings.

Eyes still closed, she rested her head on the seatback. "Oh, I'm fine. Just saying a little prayer for a safe landing." She waved off my worry.

Mirroring her idea, I rested my head on the seat back as the plane continued to bob on its descent.

My stomach lurched with each rise and fall. Luckily, it was only moments before I felt a quick jolt as the wheels touched the pavement. Clenching the arm-rest, I braced for the rapid stop.

"Safe and sound," I declared.

"Safe and sound," She echoed.

As we stepped onto the jetway, the hot, humid Florida air caught in my breath—a stark change from the already cool Iowa fall. Reaching the top of the long corridor, aromas of food and jet fuel tugged at my already queasy stomach. I breathed through a wave of nausea. A chaotic flurry of passengers and attendants packed the terminal, and I searched the crowded space for signs to baggage claim. Locating it quickly, I turned to tell Mom but realized she was no longer behind me. A wave of panic caught in my throat as my eyes immediately scanned the horde of passengers.

I cursed myself for allowing her out of my sight, even for a moment. "Where in the world did she go? How could I have lost her already? Mental note, don't let her out of your sight."

I knew if I shouted "Mom," a multitude of strangers would turn in my direction, so I began to call her name quietly.

"Vicki. Vicki. Vicki!" With each call of her name, my volume raised. I could feel the edge of alarm settle in my voice.

Everywhere I scanned, it was only strangers, most walking head down glued to their devices. Rising angst grappled at me, but why was I so worried? She was a grown woman. Though I couldn't explain it, there was something about the thought of losing her again I couldn't bear. Her small figure caught my attention near the window before I could scream her name.

"Sonya, come here!" she yelled across the terminal, her smile so wide I could see every one of her teeth. Relieved but still shaken from the ordeal, I snatched my carry-ons and stomped toward her.

"Mother, you cannot walk away from me." I pointed a stern finger in her direction. "This is a big airport, and you have no idea where you're going. You could get lost."

"Look!" She tapped the airport window, completely ignoring my scolding.

The tinted glass abated the sun's glare. I skimmed the horizon but saw nothing that might warrant her response. Everything outside was normal at a Floridian airport—a few airplanes intermingled with workers in orange vests, palm trees, and stone buildings.

"And what am I supposed to be looking at?"

Despite my bitter tone, her eyes gleamed as she pointed fiercely toward the window. "It's a palm tree! I've never seen one in real life. Can you believe it? Look, Look!"

I rolled my eyes with such intensity that there was a brief moment I feared they might lodge in my brain. Mom had nearly gotten lost in a sea of travelers, all for the sight of a palm tree. "I see it, Mom. It's glorious." My comment carried a bite of insincerity.

"Listen up, little lady, this is the first time I've seen one of these in real life, and I'm going to get excited. You should, too." When she looked at me, I could see the way the features of her face drew into genuine sympathy. "Why don't you ever take time to enjoy the view?"

A heavy fog of shame rolled over me. Why was I always in such a hurry? Why was I always rushing through life to pursue the next goal, rarely leaving time for reflection on the meaningful moments? Despite my best efforts, I couldn't seem to change that part of my personality.

"I know you're probably right, but deep-seated traits are hard to change. I've been rushing through life for as long as I can remember." I rested both hands on her shoulders. What she said was true. I knew that, but I wasn't sure when or where the need to rush to the next goal had formed. Growing up, my sister made a few wrong choices, landing her smack in the throes of an unhealthy relationship and a decade of harsh living. Though she'd worked hard to make her way out, it was a life I knew I didn't want for myself. In my young mind, the only way to avoid that trouble was to work so hard that trouble couldn't find you.

Moving my hands to her cheeks, I stared into her eyes. "I promise, at least on this trip, to take more time to enjoy the view. But, can we at least get our bags first?"

She tapped the tip of my nose, a gesture of forgiveness. "Thank you."

Feeling better about the situation, she turned toward the bustling airport for the first time, her eyes darting nervously.

Recognizing her concern, I hooked her arm in mine. "We just have to follow the signs to baggage claim. Don't worry. I'll get us there. No detours this time. Okay?"

"Okay," she winked.

*****

As usual, travelers swamped the baggage claim. Patrons crowded around the turn style for fear of missing their bag on the first round meant it was sure to be swallowed up into the bowels of the airport. Mom's eyes followed the conveyor belt, her head turning in a circle.

I tapped her shoulder. "Stand right here." I pointed to an area near the middle of the turn style. "If you see your bag, you can grab it. Otherwise, just stay right here. Okay?"

She turned to me wide-eyed. "Okay?" Her answer a question, not a statement.

A loud blast signaled the commencement of the turn style as luggage began to make its way around the loop. By the grace of God, I found my bag almost immediately. Pulling it onto the floor with a grunt, I turned back to find Mom. From the periphery, I noticed a streak of red flash into view. It was only a moment before I realized it was Mom, frantically bolting past as she zigzagged between passengers. Her elbows flung rapidly from side to side as she chased her bag around the loop, uttering condolences to innocent bystanders as she passed.

"Quick! Grab it!" Her voice was frantic.

"Mom. Mom. Calm down." I sputtered through fits of laughter. "If we don't get it now, it will come back around."

She stared at me blankly. "Oh my goodness. Why didn't you tell me?" She stopped, hand on her heart as she attempted to steady her breath. "I nearly took out a poor elderly woman back there thinking it was my only chance to get my darn bag."

"Sorry." My laughter tapered off, and I pointed to the area I'd previously left her. "But in my defense, I did tell you to stay in that spot."

She smacked a palm to her forehead. "That's just like me, always making a fool of myself."

"Don't worry. I'm sure no one noticed." We turned to look at the nearby passengers, many of whom still gaped in our direction.

"Or maybe they did." Placing my arm around her shoulders, I kissed the top of her auburn hair; the strawberry scent of her shampoo still lingered. "What do you say we get our rental car and get out of here?"

Physically exhausted, she nodded. "That sounds perfect. I'm not used to this much action. Can we get GPS this time? You know how I am with maps."

We both laughed, the sound so loud and free it reverberated in the open space.

"Yes, definitely GPS."

LIFE IS A GIFT

With my mind distracted by my secret and Mom's reliable chatter replaced with an unusual quietude, only silence filled the car as we drove to our hotel. An uneasy feeling filled my stomach, and I needed to break the silence.

"Whatcha thinking about?"

Mom's eyes, fixed out the window, remained there as she spoke. "Oh, not much, really. Just thinking about how exciting new experiences can be. There's always a little fear of the unknown," her folded hands rested on her lap, the way they did when she was reflective, "but there's a magic that's difficult to explain when you witness God's creation for the first time." She glanced at me quickly, as if to discern my response before turning her gaze back to the window. "It's like opening a present on Christmas morning to realize it's the perfect gift you didn't know you needed. There's no assembly or batteries required. You simply get to cherish it for what it is—a gift."

I stared straight out the window and allowed her words to absorb into me. Initially, Orlando seemed like any other major American city with tall buildings and interwoven highways. But on closer inspection, there was a beauty to the creation that unveiled itself as I drove. Beams of sunlight scattered off skyscrapers that jutted into the blue sky. Vibrant, verdant palm leaves waved haplessly at the mercy of the breeze while the heat radiating off the pavement created kaleidoscope ripples that emanated upward.

Digesting her words, I scanned the surroundings with a renewed appreciation.

"In one thousand feet, turn right onto Hotel Plaza Boulevard." A loud voice jerked me from my thoughts.

I jumped, the car swerving slightly. "Goodness, that woman scared me. I was knee-deep in nostalgia until she frightened it away. Maybe we should turn her down a bit."

"She's a passionate gal, isn't she?" Almost before Mom could finish, the voice boomed again.

"In five hundred feet, turn right onto Hotel Plaza Boulevard."

"All right, woman, that's enough of you." With a quick swipe of the volume knob, Charlotte, as we'd named her, was muted.

Conceding to her demand, I turned into the hotel parking lot. We'd decided earlier to spend the evening in, away from the crowded streets. The hotel was simplistic, but its quiet halls would be perfect for us. After checking in, we wheeled our bags down the long corridor to our room, where we settled our belongings into various closets and drawers.

With everything stowed away, I headed towards my bed, untucking the sheets around its entire length.

"Why do you always do that?" Her question surprised me.

I thought for a moment as I stared at the crisp white sheets dangling from the bedside, then shrugged. "I guess I don't like the way it feels when they're tightened down. I feel, I don't know. Constricted, I guess."

"Sounds about right," she mumbled, her eyes never leaving the tourism book she read as if she hadn't just assaulted my character.

"What's that supposed to mean." I snapped back, then adjusted my tone as instant regret pinged my heart. "Sorry. What I meant to say was, what did you mean by that statement?"

"Nothing bad, of course," her expression sympathetic. She walked over to my bed and sat down, patting the space next to her. "It's just, you've always hated feeling tied down. Since you were small, if anyone or anything caused you to feel threatened, you would fight back with all your might—determined to prove you were more than what anyone might think. I'm proud of your persistence, but sometimes I worry that you might be fighting too hard."

I stared at her intently, waiting for more, her expression intensifying her concern. Instead of speaking, she stared into me, seeing a place I didn't know existed. My drive and passion were traits I was proud of, and though I would be the first to admit my personality could be intense, I struggled to recognize her point.

"What's wrong with being determined or fighting for what you believe in?"

She placed her hand on my cheek. The heat warmed my skin, soothing the cold that usually resided there.

"Sunshine, there is nothing wrong with determination. What I'm saying is, you don't have to be so hard on yourself. Life isn't you versus the world. It's less about fighting and more about following, following God."

Her words pierced a place in my soul I'd long fought to hide from the view of others. Even from a young age, I harbored a sense of innate self-protection. Much older than I, my brother and sister were out of the house long before the opportunity came to play the protector. Though they tolerated me, I often spent hours alone with only books and my own words as my companions.

An overweight, introverted adolescent, I was consumed with becoming someone more than the harsh words anyone ever spoke to me. While my faith grew over the years, the notion that life could continue through an ability to follow rather than fight never crossed my mind. But hearing her say it now, I knew she was right. Life wasn't about contending with obstacles or barrages on my character. Those interferences were a regular part of existence. Life was about trusting God to guide me through every area of difficulty. It was about learning not to fight but to follow.

I rested my head on her shoulder. "When did you become so insightful?"

She wrapped her arm around me, giving me a gentle squeeze. "Just spending more time with Jesus, I guess. Your old Mom's getting pretty smart, huh?"

I huffed before I could stop it. "Well, I wouldn't go that far."

She whacked my leg. "Hey. Be nice."

"Just kidding, Mom. You have become one of the wisest people I know."

Understanding hung between us for a moment as I internalized her words, our eyes locked with the unspoken knowledge of our new bond.

Sensing the ache of truth in my eyes, she continued. "You'll get there, Sunshine. Just remember to follow God, not fight Him." She leaned over, placing a gentle kiss on my forehead. "We better get some sleep."

"I suppose you're right." I agreed.

As I pulled the crisp sheets up, her words continued to sift through my mind. I lay awake, staring into the blackness. Would I ever learn to stop fighting against life and start trusting in God's provision? Would I ever learn to see God and follow Him? It was such a difficult concept for someone like me, who'd long felt the need to fight against the cruelty of the world. Between Mom's words and the reemerging thoughts of my still kept secret, it was hours before I finally felt the peace of sleep pull at my weary mind.

Though it had taken quite some time to fall asleep, I awoke early the next morning rested and with a renewed sense of purpose and awareness. Mom's words of wisdom, 'life is a gift—cherish it,' scrolled like a banner in my mind as I moved about the room, preparing for our busy day. I knew well the deeper meaning of her eagerness for me to see every day as a blessing, never knowing when it may be your last. The mirror in front of me reflected my eyes as I stared into them, as I vowed, silently, to keep her words as a mantra.

*****

The traffic to Walt Disney World was jammed and had me on edge within minutes. Luckily, Mom's hopeful chatter lightened my mood.

"I can't wait to see Mickey. Those big fuzzy black ears and that sweet grin, I'm gonna hug him so hard." She barely paused for a breath. "And the princesses—Cinderella and Ariel. You know Ariel's my favorite." She waved her clenched fists in the air.

As we neared the park, the sign for Walt Disney World emerged overhead.

"Look, Sonya!" She squealed. "I'm here. I'm finally here!"

I laughed, free and unencumbered, releasing the tension from the night before. "Mother, you are such a kid."

"Oh, hush. Do you know how long I have waited to be here?"

My mother had a Disney movie collection that could rival most five-year-olds, and I admired her innocence. She openly preferred to watch cartoons over adult movies and purchased children's videos regularly, claiming they were for her grandchildren someday. She couldn't fool me. I knew they were as much for her as for them.

As we entered the magical world, her excitement was tangible. Awestruck eyes and a big grin permanently affixed her face. She strode with a bounce as if the concrete sidewalks had been replaced by rubber. Everywhere we turned, her anticipation renewed, and I couldn't help but feel exuberant myself.

We wove our way around the park, taking in a few rides and small shops until hunger seized our stomachs. Entering a small food court, we found a table on the edge. Consistent throughout the morning, our conversation began to subside as we ate. I noticed a tiny yellow butterfly from the corner of my eye as it swirled above my head. It fluttered and twirled for several minutes before landing delicately on my hand. Startled, I froze, afraid I might scare off my visitor. Lost in her thoughts, Mom appeared not to notice.

"Well, hello there," I whispered to the tiny creature, studying its minuscule eyes and the way the sun shimmered on its wings. "Aren't you friendly?" It rested with me for a few moments before our silence was interrupted by Mom's screech.

"Look!"

Startled out of my trance, I searched for the source of the commotion. Twenty yards away, Mickey Mouse stood with his big smile—white gloves waving as the crowd of children began to congregate. I looked back to find my winged friend. An unexpected sadness struck me when I noticed it had gone.

"Can we go see him?" She begged, hands folded in a prayer-like position.

I rolled my eyes, "Of course. Let's go see Mickey."

She approached the big-eared mouse and eagerly awaited her turn. Her excitement seemed unnatural to other adults around us, but I knew her joyfulness was her most endearing quality.

When her chance finally arrived, she stepped toward him with awe, wrapping her arms around his belly with an intensity that caught my breath. She stood back and gazed up at him with wide eyes, his fabric smile fixed as she encircled him one last time.

I knew I had to capture this moment. "Hey, Mom. Smile for a picture."

She turned for one precious photo, then, releasing herself, waved a final good-bye in his direction.

"Did you see that?" A grin swept across her face as she took my hand in hers. "I just hugged Mickey Mouse."

"Yes, Mom. I did." Something about that moment struck me. Perhaps it was the enthusiastic way she approached life, or maybe her unending joy, but her happiness seemed to settle into me, sealing up some of the broken places.

As the sun began to set on the Magic Kingdom, we wound our way toward the park exit. Being Halloween night, pumpkins were carved as characters, and orange decorations lined the sidewalks. As we sauntered past open store windows, aromas of cotton candy and caramel apples wafted toward us. Children festooned in glittered costumes trick-or-treated their way through the district. My mother, in her usual exhilaration, was transfixed by the action. Her eyes jumped wildly to keep up.

"Oh, we have to go in this one," she whisked up my arm, pulling me toward an official Disney Store. "I have to see what's inside."

"A Disney Store? Really? You know that's mostly kid stuff, right?" I ruffled her hair.

She shooed my hand away. "Never act your age."

"Well, you've got that down." I poked my elbow into her side.

She frowned, drawing the corners of her mouth down as far as possible. "I don't want to grow up anyway. Growing up is boring. Being a kid is way more fun. God wouldn't have given us all this joy in our hearts if we weren't supposed to use it."

I grabbed her, pulling her to a stop. Twisting her toward me, I looked at her with deep admiration. Eyes wide, she encompassed my hand, tugging me toward the door.

"Now that's the spirit."

Inside was a child's dream. Clothes covered an entire wall with movies around every corner. Stacks of books and stuffed animals of every character cascaded off round display cases scattered through the room. Children darted like pinballs, giddy with excitement, while nearby parents struggled not to lose them. Never had I witnessed so much Disney in one place.

"Mom, look. Stuffed..." Turning behind me, my words halted as I realized she was no longer behind me. "Not again," I mumbled, scolding myself. Then, inhaling a deep, calming breath, I quickly scanned the room, finding her, face as bright as sunshine, in front of the Mickey ears.

"Mom. Whatcha doing?"

"Oh goodness!" she grabbed her heart, obviously startled.

"Why are you so jumpy? It isn't like I shouted."

"You know how easy it is to startle me. I was engrossed in these Mickey ears. I'm trying to find my size," her expression was as serious as sin.

"Um . . . Did you just say find your size?"

"Sure did," she said proudly without a hint of embarrassment. "I've always wanted a pair of these."

Trying to remember my earlier vow to live with more joy, I decided it best to simply smile. Surveying the ears she held haphazardly in her arms, I pointed to a small set of light blue, glitter ones.

"Those. Those will match your eyes."

Pride filled her features as if she, too, could see the change. "You're right. They do match my eyes."

I stood transfixed as Mom confidently strode toward the cashier.

The cheery retiree behind the counter grabbed the ears. "Buying a gift?"

Mom beamed assuredly. "Nope. Those are for me."

The clerk squinted in confusion as I laughed behind her. Mom reached across the counter, securing her purchase. Our hearts full and bodies exhausted, we headed toward the car.

As we drove, I felt energy radiate from her as she relived the magical park. I knew each moment we spent together was a gift, and I was grateful for this time. The familiar prickle of tears stung my eyes when I noticed the Mickey ears she purchased seated atop her head.

"Whatcha smiling about, Sunshine?" Her face haloed in an orange beam, a remnant of the sun as it set along the horizon.

"Nothing, Mom. I'm just so happy to be with you again." A single tear glanced my cheek. "And those ears really do match your eyes."

THE HEARTBEAT OF GOD

I still remember my first time. A moment forever tattooed in my mind like indelible ink seeping into grey matter. It would be difficult not to remember one's initial step onto the powdered white sand, the vast dignified waves of the ocean roaring in the background. I was drawn in by the crash and pull of each crest, the sea churning in cadence with God's heartbeat. The steady rhythm of the surf as it caressed the shore was a sound heard long before it was seen.

Born in the Midwest, the largest body of water I'd ever experienced was Lake Michigan. Though alluring in its own right, the seductive magnificence of the ocean has forever overwhelmed me.

And so it was, day two of our trip, we found ourselves driving the stretch of highway from Orlando to Cocoa Beach. With the concrete road stretched before us, we watched the palm branches sway as the conversation flowed.

When we spoke, it was evident how uncanny our bond was—like an invisible connector existed between us. Our thoughts often mirrored each other before we spoke any words.

Today was no different. Between breaks in the stories, the secret I still clung to crept again to the surface. For reasons I couldn't explain, the timing still wasn't right. I hesitated a moment too long before shaking my head to clear my thoughts.

"You've got something on your mind." She paused her story to interject, her comment a declaration, not a question.

"No, I don't." I scrunched my face into my best confused look. Though my attempts to lie to her were usually pathetic, I tried anyway. I knew I wasn't prepared to share my news yet. Not here.

"Yes, you do. I know when you're thinking about something. Your eyes get all glassy like you're somewhere no one else can find you." She tucked a stray hair behind my ear, unveiling my face. "So, out with it."

I shivered, feeling exposed and vulnerable to the elements. My heart pumping in fast beats quickened my breath. I knew I couldn't continue the charade, so I offered her a small tidbit to whet her appetite. "Okay, you're right. I have something on my mind, but I'm not going to tell you yet. And no matter how hard you try, I will *not* tell you until the time is right. So you might as well stop asking."

She was physically taken aback by my tone. She stared at me, her eyes studying my face, sizing up my willpower. Years of practice meant she knew the depth of my strong-willed nature and when to choose her battles. After what felt like hours, she pursed her lips and crossed her arms in exasperation. "Fine, but you *will* tell me later, right?"

"I promise." I extended my little finger out toward her—a pinkie promise.

She curled her smallest finger around mine. "I can't wait to hear it."

I inhaled deeply and focused again on the yellow strips dotting the concrete as they flashed past me. "I promise. It'll be worth the wait."

The conversation quieted as we neared the beach as if recognizing the impact of what was to come. We wove our way through side streets, dotted with storefronts advertising the day's specials, until Charlotte, our GPS navigator, eventually led us to a parking lot a few blocks from the beach. The streets were relatively quiet on the weekday, the curbs dotted with cars. Finding a space easily, I turned the car into the parking space and killed the engine. The moment I opened the door, a shiver crossed my spine at the sound of the far-off waves. I closed my eyes as I breathed in the salty air and listened to the soft cadence of the ocean.

"Mom. Listen." I tapped my ear. "Can you hear it?"

"What am I supposed to hear?" She whispered, her eyes darted back and forth, distracted by the many tourist shops along the sidewalks.

"The waves. Listen. Can you hear them?"

She quieted herself for a moment, straining to hear the far-off sound. "I do! Where is it?"

Ahead only a few hundred feet, in front of a line of tall bushes, stood a white picket fence, its edges worn down from years of sand and sun. Next to the fence stood a sign that read "Public Beach Access." I pointed in the direction of the sign then headed toward the trunk. Retrieving the bag I'd packed with a few essentials earlier that day, I slung it over my shoulder before gesturing toward Mom to follow me.

We walked silently on the stretch of white sand toward the sea. One sight of the magnificent aqua water stopped her as if she'd been stunned. The long waves curled at their crest and created linear white lines against the turquoise water.

"My goodness, Sonya. It's incredible." I could see her eyes mist. Placing my hand behind her back, I gently guided her toward the water. The pull and retreat of the waves mesmerized us with each step.

As we neared the edge where the water and sand met, we stared into the distance. The wind blew gently across our faces as salt spray splashed our skin.

"This is one of the most beautiful scenes I have ever witnessed. It's almost like heaven." She whispered.

I turned to study her, longing to see the delicate features of her face as she spoke. Her free hand resting upon her chest rose and fell with each crashing wave. Her eyes, closed, were tilted upward toward the sky.

"There is something about its majesty that makes me feel closer to God—like I can sense Him here. Yes." Eyes still closed, she inhaled deeply, drawing in a memory. "It's the heartbeat of God."

Though we remained transfixed for minutes, I couldn't help but think about her previous comment, 'It's like heaven.' My heart ached, a mixture of gratitude and sadness as I watched her. Our relationship would never be the same, but I was eternally grateful for the time we shared now. We stayed that way, contemplating the greatness of God's creation, until Mom's voice broke our silence.

"Can I step in the water?" She questioned like a nervous child.

"Of course, you can. That's the best part."

We removed our shoes, feeling the powdered sand beneath our toes, and walked to the ocean's edge, "Be careful, Mom. The water can pull back hard, so don't go out too far."

"Okay." Her voice trailed off as she splashed, already mid-shin into the water. She squealed with excitement as each wave crashed against her body.

"Remember, don't go out too far."

"What?" The sound of the waves made it difficult to hear.

I was surprised she'd ventured as far as she had. When she was only five, an uncle threw her off a dock by the lake, trying to be funny. Not knowing how to swim, she panicked. Though her uncle eventually pulled her in, the threat of near-drowning had sworn her off swimming for a lifetime. She loved being near the water, just not submerged in it.

I cupped my hands around my mouth, hoping my warning would travel further. "I said, don't go out too far."

I gaped in disbelief when Mom ventured one step too far, and a wave slightly bigger than the previous met her short body waist-high. Despite the surprise attack, she steadied herself but underestimated the power of its retreat. As the wave pulled back toward its center, the force drug at her knees, knocking her straight to her bottom. Her arms flailed about as she fell with a splash.

Sprinting toward her, I crashed through the water and yanked her up before the next onslaught of waves threatened to bury her. Where I had expected panic across her face, there was only laughter.

"Did you see that?" She yelled, her voice high and free without a hint of alarm.

I could hardly answer. "Of course, I saw that. Are you okay? Didn't you hear me tell you not to go out that far?"

"No." She blushed. "I was so caught up in the wonder of it all."

"Goodness, Mom, you scared me . . ." Her body was soaked when I pulled her into a tight embrace.

"Oh, Sunshine. I'm fine. I feel pretty much invincible these days. But, I might not be able to say the same thing about my clothes." She looked down at her wardrobe—drenched and dripping with salt water, she wiggled her bottom. "I'm pretty sure I have sand in my panties."

"Mom, will you please stop saying 'panties.' You're making me uncomfortable."

"Well, I don't know what you want me to call them, but there's sand in there." She pointed down to her soaked underwear.

I nearly died. Spasms of laughter rolled through me like I hadn't felt in years. I welcomed them. Like a deep cleansing, they scrubbed at the layers of sadness that had long built up within me. When I finally began to settle, I looked at Mom and her mess of wet, sandy clothes.

"Goodness, Mom, I've missed you." A renewed freeness came over me in the wake of my laughter, and I allowed it to sink in before I finally spoke. "I think I remember seeing some shops where we parked that sell clothes. I bet we can get you some new ones." I turned toward our belongings, gathered near the towel on the dry sand. "On a positive note, your shoes are still dry."

"You're right," she smiled, face gleaming into the bright sunlight. "Always important to look at the positives. Now, if you don't mind, let's go get me some dry panties." She slapped my shoulder.

I shook my head. "Okay, Mother. Let's go get you some panties."

With our laughter pouring into the air, we turned toward town.

WET SKIVVIES

Tourist shops rose from the street like wildflowers lining the sidewalks. Each eclectic storefront showcased a vast array of tacky clothing, eccentric trinkets, or fine jewelry. In search of drier clothes, we maneuvered our way through patrons who now blanketed the walkways.

Jutting out from the corner of two bustling streets, a large brick building with huge windows begged for our attention. Colorful T-shirts and bold dresses obscured nearly the entire length of the glass.

I pointed to the monstrosity. "That's probably the best place to get some cheap clothing."

Distracted by the flurry of events surrounding her, it was a moment before Mom glimpsed in my direction. "Oh yes. We definitely need to go in there."

Though it was only a short distance to the shop, Mom appeared to be having a bit of trouble. Every second step, she was yanking at her shorts, swinging her leg out wide to the side.

"What are you doing?"

She snuck up close, cupping her hand to my ear. "Between these wet clothes and the leftover sand, my legs are beginning to chafe."

I pulled back, flashing her my best disapproving stare. "Mother. Really?"

"What? You asked." She snapped back, her head tilted sideways and lips pursed in retort.

"You're right. I should know better. I won't ask again." I pulled on the shop door.

A bell chimed as we entered. Vibrant tourist clothes and souvenirs bombarded our senses while incense burned centrally, filling the store with an organic aroma. A sucker for ridiculous tourist memorabilia, I leaned over and whispered a reminder to Mom, "We're just here for clothes, remember?"

"Clothes. Uh-ha. Right." The look of awe and wonder on her face contradicted her words.

"Why don't you go look for shorts, and I'll find a shirt that doesn't scream 'I'm not from around here.' When I find one, I'll come and get you."

Though her head bobbed in agreement, with her eyes darting about the store, I doubted she heard one word I said.

Bright colors and bold tie-dies vied for my attention before I noticed a rack of muted pastels in the far corner. I shuffled through the stacks of T-shirts and finally settled on a pale green with small writing near the center. Content with my find, I scanned the room for Mom and noticed she was deeply distracted by the store's collections. I knew she was in her element, so to give her some time, I began to wander.

Off in the corner was a small section of baby clothes. It wasn't a section I frequented. After being married for more than five years, parenthood was still a notion that frightened me. But I'd always been drawn to the miniature outfits. And today, the pull was especially strong. I picked up a tiny white onesie with light yellow lettering. 'Grandma's Little Beach Bum' was imprinted across the front. A warmth caressed my center. It was hard to imagine a human so tiny that it could fit inside this shirt. I held it up a moment longer before tucking the little shirt under my arm. "I suppose now's as good a time as any," I whispered.

Standing at the counter, I put my arms on my hips, trying to widen my body so Mom couldn't see what I had tucked under my arm. It was silly, but I wasn't ready for all her questions. When the cashier handed me the bag containing the onesie and Mom's shirt, I thanked her then turned to see if I could find my travel companion.

To my surprise, I spotted Mom almost immediately. She was tucked back in the corner near an expanse of purses so big they could hold a small child. Each one with a beach scene painted on its surface.

I snuck up behind her then blurted out, "What are you looking at?"

"AHH!" She screeched.

"Sonya Joy! You nearly made me pee in my pants." She panted, bent over at the waist to catch her breath. Her legs had crossed automatically.

"Well, good thing they're already wet," I said, laughing at my joke.

"Very funny. You nearly gave me a heart attack."

"Don't be so dramatic, Mom. I'm pretty sure you aren't ever going to have a heart attack." I winked.

Catching her breath, she stood up straighter. In an effort to dissuade its purchase, I ignored the monstrous purse she wore across her shoulder. Instead, I asked about the shorts she was supposed to be shopping for.

"Oh, I found a pair, but they don't have any panties."

"And, we're back at panties again." I closed my eyes, exasperated. "Seriously, Mom?"

"Payback, dear daughter." She grinned mischievously, proud of her retaliation.

"Well, I'm sure they'll dry eventually, and at least you'll have new shorts."

"Oh, even better," she chimed. "I've already checked the bathrooms. They have hand dryers, so I can just dry them there."

The image of my mother drying her unmentionables in a public restroom was almost too much. "Mom, you cannot dry your underwear in a public bathroom."

"Why not," she turned to me, truly confused.

"Because. People don't want to see that."

"They aren't going to see anything. I'm just going to put the panties under the dryer, really quick, and then put them back on." I covered my blushing face. Once she got something in her mind, short of a police barricade, there was no stopping her.

"I know I can't convince you otherwise, so I'm going to at least try and hide you." I eyeballed the large purse still hanging off her shoulder. "By the way, what is that abomination?"

"It's a purse. Don't you love it? It has this great picture of the ocean on it. I think I am going to buy it." Her voice grew more exuberant with each exclamation.

"Umm, no, I do not love it. It screams tourist. You aren't really going to buy that, are you?"

She flicked her hand toward me, waving off any concern for the judgment of others. "Of course, I am buying this purse. Why would I need to be concerned with what others think? I'm not hurting anyone. You, on the other hand, could do to remember, if you spend your whole life worrying about the opinions of others, you'll never have the courage to create the life you imagined."

I stood for a moment, letting her words drop like an anchor on my heart, securing them for the future. "When did you get so wise?" I kissed the top of her head.

"You know what, Mom? If that purse brings you joy, then you go right ahead and buy it. But can you do it quickly so we can get back to the beach?" I smiled softly.

"Sure." She started toward the counter, and then, turning back, her blue eyes caught mine. "Did you find me a shirt?"

"Yes, and I already purchased it for you. So after you check-out, meet me in the bathroom."

"Sounds like a plan." She walked away, her head bobbing to the music.

COMMANDO STYLE

M om barged into the cramped restroom carrying an oversized shopping bag stuffed to the brim. "What in the world do you have in there?" I asked.

"Nothing." She jerked her arms behind her in a weak attempt to hide her haul. The massive bag puffed out, visible from both sides.

"Look, surfers." She pointed to a dated picture of men with muscles and surfboards displayed behind me.

"Mother? Are you trying to distract me from seeing what's in *that* bag?" I reached toward it but missed as she pulled the sack further behind her.

A mischievous grin parted her lips. "Of course not. I just liked the picture?"

"You little fibber." I snatched the bag before she could stop me. "Let me see what's in there."

"Huh." She let out a sigh of defeat as I positioned the bag on the sink and began to shuffle through.

Inside was a smattering of tourist paraphernalia. Not only did it contain the new shorts and enormous beach bag she'd shown me earlier, but a picture frame covered in seashells, a light blue coffee mug with "Beach Babe" plastered on the front, two large conch shells, and a Mickey Mouse beach towel the size of a small blanket.

"What is all of this? You didn't have these when I left you." I held the mug in one hand and a conch shell in the other.

She shrugged, swaying nervously. "It's just a couple of things I picked up on my way to the cashier."

"Mom. It may look like a tourist shop threw up in your bag, but as long as it makes you happy, that's all that really matters."

She leapt forward, encircling me in a big hug. I braced against the cool dampness of her still wet clothes.

"Uh . . . Mom. You're getting me all wet."

She looked down to examine her clothes, obviously forgetting about her mishap with the ocean.

"I'm sorry, I suppose I am." Her flitted laughter echoed in the tiny bathroom, tympanic against the tiles walls.

She took one big step back and quickly jutted out her hand. "If you give me the shirt and shorts, I'll put them on. Then, since they didn't have panties, I'll come out here commando-style, and we can dry my skivvies with the dryer."

Shock struck my face. I blinked three times in quick succession. In all the years I'd known her, I'd never heard those words pass her lips. "What did you say?"

"I said, 'I'll come out here . . .'"

"Wait, wait, wait." I held up my hand, stopping her before she could continue. "I know what you said. I guess what I meant was, did you just say 'commando-style?'"

She looked at me, stone-faced. "Well, I'm not going to parade around all day in wet skivvies, which means I'm going to have to come out here 'commando-style.'" There was no attitude or harshness to her voice, just a simple statement of fact.

I shook my head, mortified. Never in a million years would I have guessed I'd find myself in this situation—a grown woman, on vacation with my mother, about to help her dry her wet underwear in a public bathroom. "This should be good," I mumbled under my breath.

I retrieved the shorts from her bag and the T-shirt from mine.

A series of grunts and groans came from the bathroom stall as she maneuvered herself into the cramped space. After a few moments, a loud bang, followed by "Ouch! Dang it," resonated from the stall.

I snorted, trying hard to hold in my laughter as I imagined the scene behind the closed door. "You okay in there? That sounded pretty loud."

"Yeah. I hit my head on the toilet paper holder when I was trying to get my darn pants off. I think that saltwater glued them to my bottom." There was a slight pause before she continued. "There's no blood, so I'm okay."

That was it. No longer capable of composure, I allowed the laughter previously percolating to freedom. Tears streamed down my face with each spasm, and my stomach ached from use. After a second to catch my breath, I managed to choke out my reply. "Well, as long as you're not bleeding." I inhaled deeply one last time to regain my composure. "Be careful in there. I'd hate to return to home and tell everyone you got a concussion from a toilet paper holder."

"Oh, you be quiet." Her muffled reply came from behind the door.

As I continued to recover, I checked my face in the mirror to ensure mascara hadn't bled down my cheeks. In the reflection, I caught sight of the bag still clutched in my hand. The weight of the purchase brought a nervous smile to my face. But, before I could get lost in thought, Mom burst through the door, disheveled. Her hair was a hot mess across her face, with strands poking out in all directions. Her face flushed with the effort it took to change clothes. She wore the new articles we had purchased, but her skivvies hung from her hands.

She twirled the wet undergarments as she sauntered toward the dryer. "Let's dry these puppies."

"Mother! What has gotten into you?"

"I'm not really sure. Just feeling kind of spicy, I guess." She snapped me with her wet underwear.

Appalled and completely confused by her actions, I gave her a gentle shove toward the dryer. "For goodness sake, Mother. Will you get over there and start drying those. I'll attempt to hide what you're doing."

As the dryer roared on, another patron opened the door into the cramped space. Unable to contain her nervous energy, Mom blurted out, "Sorry. I'm drying my panties because I fell in the ocean."

The woman, taken aback, gave her head a slight shake as if trying to comprehend what she had just heard. "Excuse me?"

"I just wanted you to know why I was drying my panties with the hand dryer. I fell in the ocean, and they don't sell skivvies here." She shrugged.

"*Mo-ther!*" My head jerked toward her. "This poor woman does not want to know why you are displaying your unmentionables. Please, just let her use the restroom." A flood of embarrassment blushed my face as I smiled apologetically in the stranger's direction. "I'm so sorry. She'll be done soon."

The woman smiled awkwardly as she walked toward the stall. My fingers tapped my forehead, a nervous habit, as I tried to imagine what she must be thinking. Waving my hand toward Mom, I encouraged her to hurry up. By the grace of God, she finished just as the woman retreated from the bathroom. I nearly shoved Mom into the empty stall, slamming the door behind her.

"Ouch, what was that for."

"Sorry, Mom, I just wanted you to hurry so we could get back to the ocean." I cringed, hoping I hadn't hurt her in my haste to get her into the stall.

I mouthed "I'm sorry," toward the stranger as she stood near me, drying her hands.

"Don't worry about it." With a dismissive wave, the woman turned and walked out of the bathroom. Just as the door began to close, I heard her giggle ring behind her.

THE SECRET

'd waited weeks for the right moment to tell Mom my secret. The nervous energy that pulsed through me made it harder to contain my news. At least now, I had a plan.

Finally, in some dryer clothes, we returned to the car, the bag of items I'd purchased pulling on my arm. Grabbing the key fob, I pressed the button for the trunk. It flung open, startling my frayed nerves.

"Geez, you're jumpy." Mom looked at me, puzzled. "Everything all right?"

Squeezing my eyes tight, I willed my mind to focus. "I'm fine. Probably still recovering from the spectacle I witnessed in the bathroom back there."

"Oh, shush." She waved off my comment and heaved her bulging bag into the trunk, then looked over at mine. "You going to drop yours off too?"

I hesitated, searching my mind for an excuse.

"Umm . . . No . . . I . . . bought a few things I want to use later, so I think I'll hold onto it." I shuddered internally and hoped my lie wasn't as pathetic as it sounded. Secrets and lying made me uncomfortable—especially to her.

"Well, I'm going to take this then." She grunted heavily, yanking her new beach towel from the bottom of the bag. "It'll be nice to sit on. I think I've had enough sand in my panties for one day."

She blurted out a loud laugh. Knowing my distaste for the word "panties," I was sure she was proud of herself for that rib. I huffed and rolled my eyes, letting her have her moment.

We headed toward the beach, the mesmerizing cadence already in my ears. As we reached an area about ten feet from the shore, we opened the bright red towel and settled into the sand. The expansive water glistened in the afternoon sun—its rays warm on our skin.

I shut my eyes, listening to the ocean's melody. Seagulls cawed overhead accompanied by the splash as they dove to the surface in search of a meal. The waves crashed rhythmically against the shore while the faint sound of a child's laughter rang in the distance. Mesmerized by the lull, I thanked God for this moment of peace.

Mom, too, sat silently next to me. In the distance, a small kaleidoscope of butterflies fluttered in the wind. Their wings flapped rhythmically as they floated on the slightest breeze. I watched their dance, transfixed by their grace.

A stiff wind blew a cool breeze off the water's surface. I heard the bag containing my item from the store crinkle gently in reply. I took a deep breath and looked up toward the pale blue sky, trying to calm the nerves that surged through me. *This is the time.*

Quietly, so as not to disturb her peaceful encounter, I whispered, "Mom."

She turned her blue eyes, piercing in the light of the sun, toward me. "Yes, Sunshine?"

"I have something I want to show you." I dug into my bag and retrieved the small onesie, handing it to her. She took the tiny article and spread it out.

"What's this? Why did you buy me a onesie," her confusion obvious.

"Read what it says." My voice shook.

"Grandma's Beach Bum," her voice trailed off as she read the final word. She sat for a moment as if trying to understand the significance. It felt like minutes passed before she turned to look at me, the onesie clutched to her. "Does this mean what I think?" Her voice cracked.

I nodded as tears formed in my eyes. I knew how long she'd waited to hear those words. Joe and I had been married for almost six years, and much to her dismay, we'd informed everyone we would wait to have children. My heart squeezed with joy as I saw her process the new information.

"Sonya," she whispered, brushing off a few stray tears. Delight sparkled across her face. "I'm so happy you finally told me."

Of course, she knew. I chided myself for thinking I could keep anything a secret from her. "I should have guessed you would already know. You see every-thing, don't you?" The corner of my lip curved upward into a half-smile.

"Yes, I knew. But I've enjoyed watching you decide how to tell me. You've made me the happiest person in the world today. I can't even tell you how long I've waited for this." Looking up toward the sky as she spoke, her words carried like a whisper in the wind. "That's a day I can't miss." She reached over to hug me, nearly tackling me in her excitement. "I love you, Sunshine. I'm so happy for you. It's going to be such an adventure."

"I love you too, Mom."

As I looked silently back over the vastness of the ocean, I caught a final glimpse of the butterflies as they fluttered away into the sun. *Quite an adventure.*

May 2013

NEVER AGAIN

learned a lot about myself over the next few months of growing pains and body changes. Most significantly was the realization I did not like pregnancy. Though many people reveled in the miracle of incubating a human—I was not one of them. My new job as a surgical Physician Assistant left me tired and swollen from standing daily for hours in the operating room. My back creaked and my feet groaned as I sunk into my bed each night. At thirty-eight weeks, I was huge and desperate for our little peanut to make her way into the world. I was convinced this pregnancy, my first, would also be my last.

What I hated most regarding my status as "with child" were ridiculous comments and foolish questions from people who should know better. I admit I've got a head full of red hair and a fiery temper to go with it. If I heard one more person ask, "Are you still here?" as if I weren't standing directly in front of them, I was going to lose my composure.

One exhausting day near the end of my term, I burst through the front door of our house, the knob crashing against the wall. "I'm going to write a book called '100 Statements You Should NEVER Say to a Pregnant Woman,' and I'm going to give it away to all of the ninnies who can't keep their mouths closed."

I slammed the door shut, rattling the mirror that hung on the wall. "It's gonna be filled with statements like 'Wow, you look like you should be due any day,' or 'You look ready to pop.' Oh, and my *personal favorite* is 'Are you still here?' *Seriously?*" I was amped up, and my voice raised an octave with each sentence. "What kind of question is that? Of course, I'm still here!" I continued, barely taking a breath.

"Then I'm going to hand it to every pregnant woman, with permission to throw it at any ignorant dingdong who can't say something appropriate." I braced myself against the wall, waiting for the blood to return to my head.

Joe stared at me, stunned. His eyes were wide with the faintest hint of fear nestled in the creases. He'd gotten used to my endless prenatal tirades, but his desperate look informed me he wasn't sure whether to stay or run.

"I've decided the only appropriate questions to ask a pregnant woman in her third trimester are 'How are you feeling, 'and 'Can I do anything to help?'" I threw myself onto the couch, huffing for air, and closed my eyes, ready to dwell in self-pity.

Joe remained silent for a moment, likely composing his words. It was at least five seconds before he made his way over to me. He placed a gentle, warm hand on my forehead. "It sounds like you had a rough day. Is there anything I can do to help?"

Well played, honey. I allowed the heat of his hand to soften my hard edges.

I filled my lungs with as much air as my swollen abdomen would allow before blowing it out in a huff. "No. Thanks for asking, though, just ready to be done with all this." I circled a finger around my stomach. "I mean, not the baby, of course, just the pregnancy part."

"I understand." He stared into me with sympathetic eyes. "Have you talked to your Mom today? She always seems to know what to say to make you feel better."

"No. But that's probably a good idea." I peeled myself off of the couch, teetering for a moment like a turtle on its back, then walked across the room to my yoga ball. Hearing somewhere it could induce labor, the large purple sphere had become a permanent fixture in our living room. Eating, watching TV, reading, I bounced.

Retrieving my phone from my pocket, I dialed her number. Her cheerful voice resonated on the other end. "Sunshine! How are you?"

"Terrible." I snarled, still bouncing. "I've tried everything I can to get this baby out. I mean every trick in the book—spicy food, acupuncture, walking, even . . . well, you know."

"I know what?"

"Mother, I am not going to say the word out loud."

"Say what word out loud?" Her blissful confusion often astonished me.

"Never mind. Let's just say if I heard it might induce labor, I've tried it." My voice shook as I continued to bob.

"What's wrong with your voice? It sounds like you're driving on a bumpy road."

"I'm bouncing on a yoga ball trying to get this baby out. Like I said, I've tried everything."

"Oh goodness, sweetheart. You know that precious little granddaughter of mine will come when she's ready. I know it's hard to see now, but God has the perfect timing for her arrival."

I knew she was right, but I did not want to hear it. I was one hundred percent over being pregnant and didn't want anyone to tell me about God's omnipotent timing. In my pregnant mind, today was a perfect day for our baby to arrive, and no one could convince me otherwise.

"Mom, I really don't want to talk about God's timing." My voice snapped back.

Silence filled the line. *Ugh. I hurt her feelings.* "I'm sorry, Mom. I didn't mean to take my frustration out on you. It's just that this pregnancy has me crazy. Can we change the subject? Maybe it will take my mind off how miserable I feel. What have you been up to lately?" I tried to raise my voice, proving my interest.

"I visited the sweatshop girls today." There was an extra perkiness in her voice. In her usual fashion, she'd already forgiven me for my snarky attitude.

Comprised of four middle-aged women, including my mother, the sweatshop was a sort of secret society. Though only the women in the group knew what really went on when the club was in session, it was common knowledge there was an abundance of laughter and shenanigans. They shared stories of life—heartwarming and tragic—and bonded over both. But through the chatter and chaos, they sewed. Over the years, my family had become the recipient of many quilts, graciously blessed by the women of the sweatshop.

"I bet that was fun. You love spending time with those ladies. What were they working on?"

I let her chatter on about a quilt they had recently finished. She described a conglomeration of all fabrics pieced together from the quilts previously given to us. Her voice gained excitement as she spoke. I listened while she laughed about her love for the companionship it brought her. My own heart lifted with her happiness, and I was thankful for the distraction.

Sensing my silence, she finally paused. "I can tell you must be tired, Sunshine. I know it doesn't feel like it now, but I promise you won't be pregnant forever."

Though I'd heard the statement before, there was something about hearing her words now that somehow uplifted me. "I know, Mom. Thanks for the reminder. Just be ready because I'm going to need you in that delivery room."

Her voice softened, almost hushed. "I wouldn't miss it for the world. Any day now, Sunshine. Any day."

June 2013

A NEW HOPE

his has to be the day.

It was three days before my due date, and my alarm blasted from my bedside table. I strained across my pregnant girth, smacking the snooze button before reclining back into my pillow. Staring up at the textured blotches of the white ceiling, I realized something about this day felt different. I couldn't narrow it down to one particular sensation, but there was a shift in the way my body felt.

Only when the alarm sounded again did I drag myself from the pillowy comfort and waddle to the bathroom. Catching my reflection in the bathroom mirror, I cringed. My hair, tangled from a restless night of sleep, poked from all sides of my head. My abdomen pressed against my pajamas, tenting them outward as I discerned the fullness around my face from the extra forty pounds I'd gained. I was unrecognizable. *Can I get any bigger?*

I rattled the thought loose. "Not today, Sonya. No more negativity." Pulling my shoulders back, I stared into my own grey eyes that cast back at me. "Today will be different."

Cranking on the shower, I waited as the heated mist filled the bathroom. When I found the perfect temperature between hot enough to melt away tension and scalding, I stepped in. With each breath, I sank into the pounding beads against my back. "Today will be different," I repeated the words like a mantra until my fingers were wrinkled and my mind was at ease. Toweling off, I went about my remaining routine. After the last swipe of mascara, I headed downstairs. Packed for over two weeks, my labor bag taunted me by the bedroom door.

"What do you think, bag? Is it time to go to the hospital?" *Goodness, I'm talking to a suitcase.* A swift kick jolted my ribcage. I flexed against it then pressed a firm palm into my baby bump. "I feel you in there. You really do need to come out. Momma's going crazy."

*****

Joe was already at the kitchen table, mind deep into the morning prayers he usually read, the last bite of waffle at his lips. Hearing me descend the stairs, he raised his eyes. His playful, half-smile framed his expression. My heart skipped. It surprised me how the curve of his mouth and the deep, piercing nature of his eyes could still arouse such a sentiment of new love. I returned his gesture, an unusual reaction lately.

"You seem different this morning." His eyebrows rose, adding a hopeful appearance to his face.

I pulled a chair from the table, plunked into it, and nestled my head into his shoulder. I inhaled a hint of his cologne and settled in deeper. "I guess I am. I really feel today might be the day. I can't explain it. I just feel different somehow. My contractions might be stronger, but I've had those for weeks." I shrugged, still unsure how to explain it myself. "It's hard to tell. Either way, I thought maybe you should put my labor bag in the car. That thing's been taunting me for weeks, and this way, I'm ready just in case."

Nine long months with me, my hormones on high, and my attitude escalated, he'd learned to say very little. Even with my improved mood, he was taking no chances. "I'll get it right now." He kissed my head before pushing back from his seat. The thuds of the chair across the tile echoed in the kitchen as he bounded up the stairs. Moments later, he descended. With my bag in hand, he headed toward the garage.

"Um. Excuse me? Aren't you forgetting something?" My voice like ice to his back, he halted mid-step. Pregnancy had sucked every bit of manners from my system.

"What did I forget? Isn't everything in here?" He held the bag up higher.

"No. Remember you have to bring the quilt from the sweatshop girls. It's not in the bag because it's too big. It was right next to it." The quilt had been recently gifted to me. Its final stitches were completed by hand at my baby shower.

"Oh yes, the quilt."

Before I could say another word, he bolted back upstairs and returned with the precious item.

*****

Twenty minutes later, my bag and quilt tucked into the trunk, Joe pulled up in front of the vast glass entrance of the hospital. The traffic in the parking lot was light this early in the morning. A few cars crawled past as people trickled in and out of the revolving door. I could still hear the far-off vibration of the recently departed helicopter. Feeling a squeeze as it pulled in my abdomen, I checked my watch. *Seven to ten minutes—still too far apart.*

My previously hopeful mood evaporated like water on hot pavement. I didn't want to be dropped off for work. I wanted to be dropped off to have a baby.

The car doors unlocked as Joe shifted to park. I struggled to turn toward him, my belly pinched against the dash. "Make sure you don't call anyone. I don't want everyone to think we might have the baby today and then be embarrassed if we don't."

Joe tilted across the seat, his smile tempering my bitter facade. "Don't worry. I won't." Sensing my misery, he settled his hands against my face. "Try to have a good day. Remember, it might feel like it, but you won't be pregnant forever."

"I know." I smiled back, thankful for his rationality.

"Why don't you talk to your Mom on the way up to work?"

Though she would invariably mention "everything will work out," or "trust in God's plan," there was a uniqueness to her delivery. She had a way of making me feel like the pieces of life were aligning just as they should.

"I think I will." I touched his cheek, soft from a clean shave. "Thanks for being so patient with me. I love you."

"Love you too. And hey?" A grin flashed his handsome face, and my heart squeezed harder. "Whether you are in labor or not, I will see *you* later."

I rolled my eyes. "Yeah, I know." I pushed against the seat as I stretched for the door. "I need a boost. Will you give my butt a shove?"

We both laughed, and I felt my chest begin to lighten. Joe placed a hand near my back and gave me a big heave. Groaning my way to a standing position, I closed the door and waved through the tinted window. I stood there, unaffected by the patients, visitors, and employees as they maneuvered around me.

As I watched his car disappear down the street, I wondered again if today would really be *the* day. Though the building had become my second home, today, it loomed before my tired feet. "Today better be the last time we meet with this baby in here." I rested a hand on my protruding belly, noticing my reflection in the mirrored glass. Then, taking a long, slow inhale, I willed myself toward the door.

*****

Entering the towering structure, I began the arduous walk across the hospital for morning rounds. Taking Joe's advice, I pulled my phone from the pocket of my white coat and dialed Mom.

"Good morning, Sunshine," her voice chipper and bright as usual. "Everything okay?"

"Oh, you know me." I sighed. "Just tired of being pregnant. When I woke up this morning, I felt like something was different, but I'm not really sure how to explain it. I've had those Braxton-Hicks contractions for weeks, but they just feel different today—*I* feel different today."

"That's promising." Though her words were encouraging, I sensed caution in her voice. She knew I was on the edge of insanity and probably didn't want to be the one to send me over. "How are they different?"

"I don't know. Stronger, I guess."

"Stronger is good!"

"Yeah, I suppose. But I've been timing them all morning, and they're still way too far apart. I don't mean to be harsh, but if this baby doesn't come out soon, I'm going to break my own water."

She paused so long I thought we'd lost the connection.

"Sonya Joy." My name came slow and hushed. "You wouldn't dream of doing such a thing? You could hurt yourself or the baby." Her voice quieted further. "You can't really break your own water, can you?"

"Mother, your innocence is endearing. I cannot and will not break my own water. I'm just frustrated with the duration of this pregnancy. The last thing I want to do is go to work today and listen to more people ask me if 'I'm still here.' I mean, of course, I am. They're looking at me, right? At least, that's what I want to say." My shoulders slumped with the reality of another day of pregnancy.

"Oh, Sunshine. I'm sorry you feel so miserable. You know I would take it from you if I could." It was a sentiment she meant fully.

"I know you would, and I sincerely appreciate the offer."

"I'm sure you don't really want to hear this, Sonya, but you know this will all work out in God's time. He knows when the moment is right. You need to remember to trust in His timing. Besides, from the sounds of how you're feeling, His timing might just be today."

I knew what she said was the truth, but my pregnancy hormones had me ratcheting up the 'I don't want to hear about God's time scale. I considered hanging up but knew better of it. "I know. Thanks for the pep talk. I still just can't help the feeling that something's different." Reaching the tower of patient floors, I pressed the small silver button. The elevator dinged, and the metal doors parted. Pressing the button for my floor, I turned back toward the door, watching as they closed me in. "I think I might go over to the labor floor after rounds and just make sure everything's okay."

"That sounds like a good idea. It might make you feel more at ease."

"Or more disappointed," I grumbled.

I knew before she said it that she wanted to make everything okay. From as early as I could remember, she'd made it her life's mission to protect us from any pain she could.

"Sunshine. Before you know it, you'll be holding that precious little miracle in your arms and forget all about how miserable you feel. If we didn't forget, none of us would ever have had more than one child," she chuckled. "Let me know what you hear from the maternity floor. Okay?"

"Okay. And Mom?"

"Yes, Sunshine?"

"Thanks for listening to me vent."

"I'm here with you always, don't ever forget that."

"I know." I closed my eyes, recognizing the weight of her statement.

As the phone disconnected, wetness stopped my steps. I stood paralyzed. It hadn't been the gush I'd expected, but nonetheless, a sensation I'd never experienced. *Did my water just break? Shouldn't I know if my water broke? This pregnancy is really starting to mess with my mind. I better have this baby soon, or they will have to put me in the psych ward instead of the maternity ward.*

I called my co-workers to inform them I would be late. "No, I am not in labor—at least I don't think so. I just feel like I need to get checked out. I'm sure I'll be back to work soon."

When the elevator opened, I pressed the down button. Feeling the rush of air as it pushed toward the floor, I shivered against the cool draft. As the doors parted, I started my waddle across the hospital to the maternity floor.

TRUST ME

"**W**ell, I'm not sure what you felt, but it wasn't your water breaking," the bright-faced nurse informed me from the bottom of a sheet that spread over my knees.

"Well, this is awkward," I mumbled so she couldn't hear.

"Ok, thanks for checking." I tried to sound chipper but knew the shake in my voice betrayed me.

Defeated and embarrassed, I heaved myself off the bed and dressed as quickly as my huge belly would allow. Minutes later, I pushed through the big metal doors, more distraught than ever. Plunking into a chair meant for waiting family, I stared blankly ahead. An expanse of windows reflected the hot June sun and humidity sat thick in the air distorting the landscape beyond the hospital.

"I can't go out there again. I can't face another day of ridiculous comments and constant pain. I think I'll plant myself in this chair and wait until my labor starts." I said to absolutely no one.

Trust in my timing. The voice came like a whisper in my ear. I glanced behind me, half expecting to see someone.

There was no one.

Trust in my timing. The soft inflection continued from my heart as a cool shiver ran through me. I knew what was happening. This was how I always heard His words, a gentle voice followed by a flutter through my skin. This was God's voice.

Beyond the horizon, the heat rippled across the landscape, and I let the words become a part of me.

Trust me.

Could I do that? Could I let go of my plan long enough to trust the One who created me and the new life inside me? He'd proven himself before, not that He had to. Could I finally learn that it was easier to trust and wait than to operate on my own agenda?

From the table next to me, the sweet smell of the fresh flowers infused my senses. With each inhale, I pushed the words further into my soul, allowing them to take up residence there. Still erratic and unsteady, the contractions pressed against my abdomen until I lifted my eyes toward the sky. "Okay. I'll trust your timing. But if you wouldn't mind hurrying up."

A glance at my watch showed how late it'd become. My phone began to vibrate, and I pulled it from my pocket, noticing "Mom" on the display. I held it for a moment without answering. I didn't want to talk, but if anyone could help, it was her.

"Hey, Mom," my voice deeper in depression.

"Uh, oh. Didn't go well, huh?"

"No, false alarm." My voice shook as I attempted to hold back the tears that stung my eyes.

"I'm so sorry, Sunshine. Sooner than you know, you'll be holding your precious baby girl, and you'll forget all your pains. But, for now, go back to work. It'll help take your mind off everything. Remember, focus on the outcome. When we fix our minds on the goal, it makes the journey more tolerable."

Trust me. The voice responded.

"Okay, I got it. Trust you." I said out loud to His voice in my head.

"Huh?"

"Oh, nothing. I think I'm hearing things. You're right. I'm gonna head back. I can't really walk and talk anymore, so I'll call you later."

"Okay, Sunshine. Love you."

"You too, Mom."

With a renewed lightness in my step, I headed down the steps, focused on the baby I would hold very soon, and a trust in the One who had created her. After all, Mom was right. Work would be just the distraction I needed.

*****

By noon my contractions had grown intensely and pulsed every five to six minutes. Though I assumed I was in labor, I refused to step back into the delivery floor until there was no doubt I was leaving without a baby. We were set to operate that afternoon, and I resolved to continue my routine until I could no longer handle the pain.

As we dressed for the OR, I was terrified my water would break during our case. I whipped a mattress-size maxi pad from my locker and secured it in my underwear. Hoisting the green scrubs around my protruding belly, I winced as another contraction rolled through.

Climbing the flight of stairs, I reached the scrub sinks panting and out of breath.

"Hey, there." A chipper, familiar voice emerged from behind me.

I turned to find Dr. Denny's tall thin frame. "Whoa." He pointed at my belly.

Here we go again. Another smart comment. Wait for it.

"When are you due?"

I closed my eyes so he couldn't see them roll, then practiced my best fake smile. "Two days. So really, any day now."

"Huh. I would have guessed that. You look like you're about ready to pop."

And there it is, folks. I looked for something to throw at him but found nothing.

"Sure do." I hoped my voice sounded as annoyed as I felt. I was tired of being polite. Breathing through another contraction, I spun back to the scrub sink.

"Well, good luck." He called as he hurried down the hallway.

After rinsing my hands under the running water, I scrutinized the soap as it swirled down the drain. "I wish I could just disappear. Sure would be easier than facing these people." With water dripping from my arms, I jammed my elbow into the door handle and trudged into the OR. I cast my eyes on the back wall but couldn't ignore the sympathetic glances from each person in the room. Putting on my gown and gloves, I secured the ties for what I hoped would be the last time until after this baby was born. A quick check of the clock confirmed each pull came in perfect succession. Despite their steady squeeze, I still felt no other signs of the baby's arrival.

After finishing the surgery, I tore off my gown and dumped it in the trash. I skirted through the door before anyone could stop me. Midway down the white hallway to the recovery room, something changed. My contractions pulled deep across me, stopping my breath.

"I think I need to go," I said to my friend Charley, the surgeon I assisted for over two years, who had now reached my side.

"Oh." His brown eyes widened. A father himself, he knew the look. "Okay. Yeah. Do whatever you need."

As my steps began again, I heard his voice once more. "Don't forget to let us know how you're doing."

I pivoted back toward him. "I will. Thanks."

Exiting the OR hallway, I fumbled for my phone and punched in Joe's number. He answered on the second ring. I spoke before he could. "I'm going to the delivery floor. I think I'm in labor."

"Really?" His excitement electric through the speaker.

"I think so. My contractions are every four minutes, and they really hurt."

"Okay, I'll be there as soon as I can." I knew it would take him some time to secure another faculty member to monitor his classroom. First labors were notorious for taking their time, so I figured it would be a while before I required his assistance anyway. Ending the call, I returned my phone to my pocket.

The usual, tolerable walk across the hospital was daunting with my more frequent contractions. My body strained as each one rolled through, making me pause my steps. Not wanting to worry passing visitors, I inhaled sharply until the spasm released.

Reaching the big metal doors of the labor and delivery floor, I pressed through them. I took one look at the nurse behind the desk as another contraction gripped. *Today is the day. Praise God. This is it.*

JUST BREATHE

At twice the size of a regular hospital room, the delivery suite felt comfortable, uncramped. Monitors and cables flanked both sides of my bed, and a spotlight hung from the ceiling. Large windows across one wall filtered light in, one beam spreading across my bed.

Joe reached the hospital just as my nurse had me settled in. He laid my bag in the corner next to a small couch that could be used for sleeping and draped the quilt on top.

"You can bring that over here." I patted the space beside me.

He tucked the quilt by my side.

"How are you doing?" Creases of worry pressed into his forehead.

"Not too . . ." The pain cut off my last word.

Without hesitation, he joined my side, leaning in so far that he nearly fell into the bed.

"I'm good." I inhaled sharply, blowing off the discomfort. "I think it's time for my epidural."

From the moment that the two small lines appeared on my pregnancy test, I knew an epidural was in my labor plan. I didn't like pain. Though I greatly respected women who had given birth naturally, I did not want to be one of them unless they gave out rewards or gobs of cash. Feeling the pressure of another contraction pull down against me, I pressed the button for my nurse.

"Can I help you?" A voice vibrated through the speaker.

"Can you please call for my epidural?"

"Of course," she replied cheerily.

Shades of purple and pink shone through the window as the sun began to lower its way across the watercolor sky. As I waited for the anesthesiologist, I caught Joe searching my bag. The hands of the clock on the wall indicated what my belly already knew.

"There aren't any snacks in there because I knew I couldn't eat them. You could get some at the cafeteria." I could tell he was starving. Being a gentleman, he tried not to say anything.

"I promise, I'm not even hungry."

"What if you have the baby while I'm gone? I'd feel terrible." His face curled into a pout.

"Joe, please go get something to eat. I promise to hold her in until you get back." We both knew even if I could, I wouldn't. Nonetheless, I reassured him. "Seriously, please." I swished my hand toward the door, gesturing for him to go.

His relief was immediate. He planted a soft kiss on my forehead before turning toward the door. "Okay. But just a snack. I'm really not *that* hungry."

"Uh, huh." We both knew he was going to eat more than a snack. He blew me a final kiss and escaped out the door.

Silence filled the room in his absence. A chill shook my body, precipitated by the cool liquid that dripped into my vein. My IV hung from the tall metal pole, just in front of the monitors connected to my abdomen. The round light that hung from the ceiling reminded me of those we used in the OR, only smaller. It was awkward and disconcerting to be on the patient side of medicine. I was used to being the provider.

With the cold settling into my bones, I spread the quilt over me. Between sessions of contractions, I found myself staring out the enormous tinted glass windows. Following an intense contraction, I noticed a butterfly fluttering on a breeze. I followed its performance before it flew off with another flick of the wind. In the same instance, I heard a knock at the door.

"It's just me, Sunshine. Can I come in?"

"Mom." In my hormonal state, the sound of her voice broke my brave veneer. As she neared me, I lost it. Every bit of composure I'd worked so hard for, to be the strong-willed, tough as nails woman I'd grown into, washed away with the look of love and concern that settled into her face. She wrapped me in a generous hug as my tears rained onto her shoulder.

"Mom, it's really starting to hurt, and I'm getting scared." As if on cue, another contraction rolled its way down my abdomen, the pain growing more intense as it radiated toward my lower back.

I was so tired. I had been a fighter all of my life, not physically, of course, but emotionally. I always fought against the bullies or the belief that someone successful couldn't come from a small farm town and two parents with no college education. Fighting the death of people I loved and dreams, I'd always attached to them. And I didn't want to fight anymore. I wanted to be the little girl that sat in her mama's lap, knowing everything was going to be okay.

"Oh, sweetheart. I'm here now." Her breath was warm on my ear as she whispered. Though the pain remained, an instant surge of peace replaced the chill previously coursing through my body, and I stayed there for a moment, wrapped in my mother's arms. I allowed her honey scent to soothe the pain.

As the contraction receded, I lifted my head from her shoulder, taking in her face. My continuous beacon of safety, she drew me in. Her presence surrounded me, and I could feel my breath begin to settle. Feeling my body relax, she searched the room. "Where is Joe?"

"I'm right here." His voice called from the hallway. "I went on a quick snack run, but I'm back." He was slightly out of breath as if he'd just run up the stairs.

My mother chuckled and glanced my way. Her mouth curved upward, tucking into a smile. We had an uncanny way of communicating entire conversations without ever saying a word, all sentiments spoken by the look in our eyes and expressions on our faces.

Snack run? She raised an eyebrow.

Yup. My lips pursed silently. I started to laugh, but it caught in my throat as another contraction gripped me.

Before the pulling sensation passed, the anesthesiologist knocked at the door. Following a brief introduction, he worked to place the epidural into my spine. With a quick pinch, the relief was almost instant.

"Thank you," I whispered, exhausted.

"You're welcome. Just let the nurse know if anything changes."

I thanked him again as he exited.

The nurse returned me to the appropriate position in bed before Mom chimed in. "You feeling okay, Sunshine?"

"Yes. Less pain right now, just a little ache in my back. Did you ever have an epidural?"

"With you, yes. Your head was so big I almost had to have a C-section."

The nurse giggled from the corner.

I twisted to see her, winking. "Mother. You don't always have to tell that story."

"Oh, I suppose I don't. It was just *so* big."

"Mother!" I interjected, my embarrassment escalating.

"What? I thought it was interesting that I didn't have any trouble pushing out your brother or sister. Their heads were more normal size, I guess."

Joe let out a snort from the couch in the back of the room.

"Really, honey." I squinted my eyes, staring him down.

"What? It was funny." His tone was hushed by the steeled look on my face. "I'm sorry. I'll just keep to myself over here." He shifted his eyes downward.

I pivoted back to Mom. "Okay. We get your point." My words were snotty. "Sonya had a big head when she was born. You can stop talking about it now."

"Oh, honey. I'm sorry. I wasn't trying to embarrass you. I'll hush up."

"No, I'm sorry. I'm sensitive today." I hung my head, disappointed. "Usually, I can take a joke better."

We continued to converse idly for the next few minutes. Though my epidural eased the pain, I could still feel every contraction's pull. Something was wrong. A deep boring pain had taken hold of my back and had only increased as we talked.

"Joe? Could you come over here? I think something's wrong."

Surging from his spot by the window, it was a split second before his hand reached mine. "What do you mean?"

"I'm still feeling a lot of pain in my back. Can you please call the nurse and ask her to come in?"

Frantically, he searched the bed from my call button. He pressed it, lighting up the little red button. The pain continued to heighten, intensifying my every nerve. When the nurse arrived, I pleaded with her to fix whatever wasn't working.

As she quickly surveyed the lines, her eyes betrayed the calm in her voice. "I'll call anesthesia to see if there is anything they can adjust. But you're pretty far along, so they may not be able to help."

Her final words shot off like a starting gun. Every sensation intensified. Tears streamed down my face as the pain racked my body. "Why isn't this working? I need an epidural that *works*. I didn't want natural labor. Now I have numb legs, and I can't move. Ouch. OUCH!"

Another contraction roared through my body. "I can't do this," I screamed.

Joe held one hand and my mom the other. "Sweetheart, you can do anything. Anything you put your mind to. I have witnessed you pull through challenges far greater than this. Joe and I will be right here. You know I would take your pain if I could. Just breathe." Her voice was medicinal to my aching body.

I inhaled deeply, pleading with anyone to help me. Exhaling as another wave passed, two doctors and a nurse entered through the door. The anesthesiologist looked at me somberly.

"Unfortunately, you're too far along to try another epidural, but I can try a higher dose of the medication to see if that helps."

"Anything. Please. Try anything." I begged through whimpers of pain, embarrassed at my weakness.

After manipulating flow rates and adding a boost of the pain medication, the anesthesiologist left the room. Within minutes, it was clear that the changes he made were of no help.

Between thrashings of pain, Mom whispered in my ear. "You can do this. You're so strong."

Trust me. The voice echoed within me again.

I gazed up at her, and something shifted in my brain. No longer was I focused on the pain but the end result. In a short time, I'd be holding my precious baby. I shifted toward Joe. "Let's do this."

The pain was my motivator. In every shudder, I pushed with any ounce of force I could. The agony continued with fierceness. The lull between contractions, now only brief, provided little rest. I heard the nurse mention the baby's heart rate, but I was too exhausted to comprehend her statement. As I breathed into one final push, my baby girl emerged.

I felt the pressure and pain, then instant release. They placed her briefly on my chest until it became obvious something was wrong. Terrified, I gripped the bed as they carried her limp blue body away from me, my eyes trained on her. It was as if the whole world went silent. Trying not to scream, I turned to Joe. "She isn't crying. Why isn't she crying?" Dread surged through my body as I remained helpless and immobile in my hospital bed.

"I don't know why, Love. They're working on her." A team of doctors and nurses rubbed and manipulated her flaccid blue body.

I threw my head against my pillow. "God, she isn't breathing. She has to start breathing. Please help her. You told me to trust you, and I'm trying, but not this. Please don't take my baby, too." Fear gripped my body as I pleaded for my newborn's life.

Even seconds can feel like an eternity when what you're facing is possible death. I couldn't breathe. It was as if the whole room had frozen in time. A loud, vibratory hum rushed through my head, broken only by Mom's whisper, "She's going to breathe, Sonya. Listen."

A moment later, a loud cry shrieked across the room. A rush of pink flooded her body as her lungs breathed life. A wave of relief crashed over my body, and heavy tears of gratitude dripped down my face. I sank into Joe's shoulder.

The doctor's voice interjected. "She's had a bit of a tough morning. Her heart rate began to increase toward the end, which means she likely has an infection. I think we better take her down to the nursery and get everything examined. You'll be able to see her soon, but we'll need to get you fixed up first."

The nurses settled my swaddled baby into the bassinet. Before they could leave, I grasped for Joe. "Go with her." My heart longed to go to, magnetized by the unbreakable bond of motherhood. But I remained locked by my numbness, prisoner to my hospital bed.

"Are you sure?" His eyes were torn.

"Yes."

Before they left, one of the nurses turned back. "Do you have a name yet?"

I peered up at Mom. So much of my life, my journey to this moment revolved around the soul inhabited in her depth. I locked eyes with Joe as he nodded a silent *yes.*

Her name is Lillian. Lillian *Victoria.* Just like her Grandma."

REDEMPTION

"Good morning, Sunshine." Mom's voice was bright on the other end of the line—too chipper for eight a.m.

"Obviously, you didn't get woken up four times last night by a screaming baby," I muttered in my haze of exhaustion.

"How's everything going today?" It was standard for her to check in on us daily since Lillian was born, and even though I complained, I secretly loved hearing her voice.

We'd been in the Neonatal Intensive Care Unit, or NICU, for six long days, and I ached for the day we would go home and settle into a more normal routine. Peeling myself from the vinyl hospital couch, I walked to where Lillian lay sleeping in her bassinet. Still connected to a slew of wires, she appeared to be generating electricity they were trying to harvest. *Maybe I could use the money to pay for this hospital bill.* I chucked at the thought. Placing my hand on her head, I avoided the IV jutting from her scalp. After multiple attempts at other locations, it was their last resort.

"We're okay." I longed to hold her, to feel the warmth and signs of life that pulsed from her tiny body. But I knew that might wake her. Given the nights we'd been having, I opted instead for the chair beside her. "We still have one day of the IV antibiotics left, but she's doing really well. The nurses keep telling us she's the healthiest baby on the floor."

Over a week had passed since Lillian was born with her entrance as dramatic as her personality—blue with the cord wrapped around her neck. The prize for such an arrival? A seven-night stay in the NICU. The nurses were magnificent, but between no sleep, postpartum hormones, and a baby that refused to nurse, I had begun to question my sanity.

"It sounds like my granddaughter is doing remarkably well considering her start. She probably has a flair for the dramatic—like her mother." Her comment trailed off at the end as if she were afraid I would hear it.

I could be dramatic, but not in the fancy clothes and the overacting kind of way. No. My drama centered on perfection and a need to control. In my mind, I knew what was best, and no one was going to change that. I wasn't proud of my character flaw, and I worked hard to change it. But didn't everybody have their shortcomings?

"Ha. Ha. Proud of yourself for that one aren't you?"

"Yeah, kind of." What started as a giggle gained steam and roared into a full-fledged laugh. Long, bright, and full of life, it was infectious. It wasn't what she said, but the free, unadulterated way she laughed with a joy that tickled my soul. Before I knew it, I found myself following suit. Feeding off each other, we carried on until Mom snorted and I nearly peed my pants.

"Phew. That was great." I waited as she let out a few straggling chuckles. "Thanks for that. But anyway, I didn't call to pick on you. I wanted to see how you were doing?" She had an eerily accurate sixth sense when it came to my feelings. Like a prize-winning bloodhound, she could sniff out disappointment with true skill.

"I don't know. This mother thing is harder than I thought. We don't seem to be clicking. It doesn't help the only time I'm allowed to hold her is when she's attempting to nurse. It's like my breasts repel her. Every time I try, she screams until I put a bottle in her mouth. I've had so many nurses and lactation consultants here the last few days, I feel like a heifer at the dairy farm." I snorted, trying to make light of a difficult situation. Though I'd tried for days to make nursing work, its stress seemed to worsen, rather than support our new bond.

"Not every mother is cut out for breastfeeding, Sonya. You and your siblings were all formula-fed and turned out just fine. Give it an honest try, but if it doesn't work out, don't judge your worth as a mother on one aspect in a long journey. I want you to spend more time holding your baby than fighting her. If she's anything like you, she's going to be a little stubborn."

Snuggled soundlessly in the corner of her crib, Lillian seemed not to notice our conversation. Her face was angelic, her pillowy cheeks squished against pink pouty lips. Seeing my baby sleeping peacefully next to me, something inside me shifted. The true meaning of motherhood wasn't about nursing, diapers, or NICU stays; it was all about one thing—love.

"You're right. I'm sure things will be better once we get out of here and can head home to a normal routine. Whatever that looks like."

"Oh yes. It will be infinitely better. Say, did they ever figure out why she got an infection?" Sometimes conversations with my mother changed directions so quickly that they gave me whiplash.

"Not really. There's a risk with any delivery, but they did tell me it was good that I got her out quickly. Since the cord was wrapped around her neck, the outcome could have been much worse. I guess it was a blessing my epidural didn't work well. It forced me to push her out faster."

"That's a God thing." Without physically seeing her, I knew Mom had placed her hand gently against her heart, as she did every time she spoke of her beloved Father.

"I love how you call any act of fortunate coincidence a 'God thing.'" My tone bordered on sarcasm. Though I'd always considered myself a believer, in my post-hormonal state, it was difficult to see how the God who loved me so much and had asked me to trust Him could determine this blue baby and a NICU stay was a God thing.

"God doesn't create simple coincidences, Sonya. He creates experiences—exactly how they're meant to be. You'll know when you've encountered such a moment. You'll feel it in your heart. An event that fits together too perfectly to be an accident—that's a God thing." I looked to Lillian, her breath rising and falling with perfect ease. My perfect little miracle. What was more important, how she entered the world, or the simple truth she now lay next to me, days from coming home? That question was likely to take a while to answer.

"You're right, Mom. It's difficult to see any situation as 'meant to be' when you're trudging through it, but if I'm honest, I feel a little cheated out of the normal newborn experience. Whatever that looks like."

I wanted an infant I could snuggle in my labor room, snap pictures of without being covered in wires, then two days later, buckle into a car seat and take home. But it wasn't meant to be. And now, within the stark confines of a hospital room, I listened to the regular beep of the monitor, wishing I had delivered a "healthy" baby.

Then, like a whisper from within, I recognized the truth of it all. My delivery, and the days to follow, may not have been as I had hoped, but my baby was here, alive and breathing. There were women I knew, friends and acquaintances, who never had the blessing of bringing their baby home. The thought caused guilt to rise up within me, churning my stomach.

"Oh, Sunshine. I know you feel a void, but our suffering has a purpose. Even experiences perfectly created by God can be undeniably difficult. They're faith testers. But when we keep pressing on through the difficulty, not only will God bring us through the hardship, He'll make us stronger on the other side. You'll see. Someday God will use your story to ease the suffering of others. And then you'll find your 'why.'"

A silence crossed between us as I internalized her statement. Her wisdom surprised me, despite her difficult upbringing and naive view on life. Like many others, I'd endured times of great suffering—loss and grief so suffocating that I feared I might never surface again. In my agony, I looked to God and pleaded, "Why? What is the purpose of all this?" I never thought my suffering might be intentional or that my pain might someday help relieve someone else's. Even more, that it would serve a greater purpose beyond my imagination. My eyes lifted, fixed on a cloud that wisped through the sky. Her words fell on me like snowflakes on the flat ground. *Could there really be a greater meaning for all of our heartache? Our pain? Could it all be an intentional part of a grander plan?*

"Sunshine?" Her words broke through my trance.

I shook my head, releasing the thought. "Sorry. I got distracted for a moment. I've never thought of my pain that way—that there might be a lesson for my heartbreak. I believe in God's infinite wisdom as much as you do. I just wish it was more in alignment with mine."

"Of course you do. Don't we all? But we could never orchestrate a plan as perfect as God can. We can't see far enough in the future. Suffering and pain might feel unbearable at times, but they often serve as turning points in our lives. In the midst of our heartache, it can be difficult to see. But remember, nothing is a coincidence. We have to learn to trust in the Ultimate Planner. We can choose to be angry, or we can choose to find courage through faith and trust."

The peace and grace of her wisdom burrowed into my heart as I sat silently, cherishing the new life that lay beside me. "That's beautiful, Mom. I guess it's just hard to see the sunshine when you're in the midst of the storm. I think I underestimated the power of these postpartum hormones."

"They are something, aren't they? I remember. There were moments after each of you was born I didn't even know myself. I would sob over nothing. I cried so uncontrollably over a Hallmark movie after you arrived, I thought Dad was going to ban me from ever watching one again." She laughed, effervescent, breaking my somber mood.

"Sounds like I have a lot to look forward to. So far, motherhood has consisted of inflatable donut cushions, cracked nipples, and uncontrollable crying. It's glorious."

"Oh, Sunshine. When you get home in your own space, everything will be different. You'll have the comfort of your bed, and so will Lillian. Until then, concentrate on snuggling your baby and get some rest. I love you so much."

The melodic tone of her voice reverberated in my heart. I never wanted to take for granted the blessing of her love, a gift to be cherished.

"I love you, Mom. I'll talk to you again soon."

As our conversation ended, I recalled her words. Maybe she was right. Perhaps my hardship now, and every past or future incident of heartbreak, was meant to make me stronger and serve a far greater purpose than it appeared on the surface. Though only time would tell, the promise of redemption for my suffering was a comfort I would hold onto for a long time.

I sat in the sterile surroundings of the NICU, staring out the window. In the distance, a striking view of downtown rose out of the horizon. The golden dome of the Iowa capitol sparkled in the sunlight. Clouds passed freely, undisturbed, while verdant leaves swayed slightly in the gentle breeze. Lost in thought, my awareness was brought back to reality by His voice.

Trust me. I felt His delicate words, once again, as I closed my eyes reverently and tilted my head against the chair. "I know. I know…"

RETURN POLICY

s there a return policy on tiny humans? I couldn't fight the thought as I laid my swaddled, finally silent, baby into her crib.

We'd been home from the NICU for almost two weeks, and despite Lillian's cuteness during sleep, her incessant, constant, ear-piercing cry had me sinking into a dark place.

"Mom." I poured my woes into the phone. "What's wrong with her? She won't stop crying. Day, night, hungry, fed, all she does is scream. You said it'd be better when we got home. But it's not. It's worse." My cry catapulted into hysterics as I sank my head into my free hand.

How had I gotten to this emotional state? Hormones? Lack of sleep? This was my baby that I was talking about returning to a store, like a shirt you tried on at home and decided you didn't like. Wasn't it supposed to be all sweet snuggles, powdery smells, and hearts bursting with joy? I wasn't experiencing any of those. "What is wrong with me?"

Her voice was gentle, as if afraid she might chip away at my remaining composure. "Sunshine, I'm so sorry." Her voice soothed like ice on a burn. "Some babies cry a lot for no real reason—it's colic. Your sister had it, too. It feels unbearable, but Lillian will eventually grow out of it."

"I don't . . . care what *it's* . . . called . . . I can't . . . do . . . *it* . . . anymore." Each word choked out between desperate cries.

There was a short silence on the other end as she waited. She knew what I needed—time for my tears to flood like water released from a dam. All the pain in my heart, the delivery, Lillian's traumatic entry, the NICU stay, it all rushed out attached to the tears I now shed. I stayed there, head in hand, crying from my deepest places until my body slumped with fatigue onto the couch. Only after my sobs began to fade into quiet spasms of breath did Mom continue.

"I know it's hard. But believe me, once Lillian grows out of it and gives you her first smile or coo, your heart will be so full you'll wonder how it could possibly fit in your chest. I can't imagine my life without you kids."

"You're so much stronger than you think, Sonya. Sometimes life requires us to dig in during the most challenging parts and lean on those who love us—me, Joe, God. I know you don't feel like He's there right now, but He is. And He's using this situation for good. I promise you."

My rational mind wanted to believe her. My determined, Type-A personality had overcome incredibly challenging obstacles, using them as momentum to achieve outcomes beyond my expectations, and I'd seen others do the same. When a long-term relationship ended in college, I was devastated. Though the end had been a long time coming, rather than fall into despair, I used it as a catalyst to prove I was stronger than anything life could throw at me. Motivational quotes and Bible verses I'd scrawled on note cards were my constant reminders of God's love and plan for my prosperity—not the pain and rejection I felt. His words became my driving force away from pain and into my new future.

Hearing Mom's reminder now somehow ignited the same passion to overcome, and I felt a peace begin to discharge from my being like an internal beacon of light. *I know God. Your plan. Always your plan.*

"Are you still there?" Mom's question interrupted my thoughts. My introspective travel down memory lane, stealing my attention.

"Yes, I'm here. I just got lost in a memory for a moment. You're right. There are moments between episodes of screaming when she is snuggled into me, and I can feel the love you describe. She's a part of me and a blessing regardless of her difficulties. Perhaps, someday, I will be able to use this for good—just like you said."

Lillian grunted from her crib, and I rose from my slump on the couch. Walking to her, I studied her like one would a precious, unbelievable gift. Her skin, new and soft, shimmered in the nearby sunlight. For a brief moment, I sensed an optimism that wasn't there before.

"That's exactly right, Sonya. You can get through anything. When you can't rely on your own strength, remember, you have God within you. Not around or near you, *within* you."

What Mom said was true. No matter how difficult the situation seemed, I didn't have to rely on my own strength. I had God within me, and He was strong enough.

Despite Lillian's sleep, I needed to hold her. She was a part of me that had been missing. I lifted her gently, praying not to wake her. The amount of warmth from her tiny body surprised me as I tucked her into my neck, her sweet fragrance melting into me. "We're going to get through this, baby girl. Momma loves you."

With delicate ease, I sank into the nearby recliner and began to rock, noticing just how much she resembled Mom—plump round cheeks and button nose, the curve of her fingertips, and the shape of her fingernails. Resting my head against hers, I closed my eyes in silent prayer.

Thank you, Lord, for this precious gift. I know she was sent here for a purpose. Though this time is difficult, with Your help, we can conquer any obstacle.

October 2013

TORI

"**M**other, what in the world are you wearing?"

It was Halloween night, and I'd propped up four-month-old Lillian in her Bumbo chair. Too cheap to spend thirty dollars on a costume she'd only wear once, I'd fashioned a ghost outfit from a white onesie, stitching on felt black circles for eyes. With cool temperatures forecasted, I decided it was best we stayed snuggled in the warmth of the house. Knowing how much she loved spending time with the baby, I'd invited Mom.

To say I understood my mom was an understatement. From the time of my youngest memory, my mom was my most constant companion. Since I'd been old enough to remember, my mother's had the spirit of a child. Children gravitated toward her as if they could sense she was one of them. Laughter, joy, and a fierce love of family had dominated her being, and it was difficult to fathom how she'd grown to be so lighthearted given her troublesome youth. I resolved to dive deeper into her past but knew this wasn't the time. Despite our deep bond, nothing could have prepared me for what was situated before me.

Mom glanced down at her outfit, smoothing her hand along the surface, her face giddy. "Don't you love it? It's so fuzzy and festive." Her expression brightened as she swirled the fur with her fingertip.

"Fuzzy, yes. Festive?" I raised a skeptical eyebrow. "I'm not sure *festive* is the right word. At your age, ridiculous sounds more accurate. You're dressed as a Care Bear." She was a vision in soft yellow fur that covered the entire length of her body like adult footie pajamas. On her tummy was the signature circular Care Bear emblem. "Where did you buy that thing anyway?'

Ignoring my snide remark, she persisted. "I found it online. I even figured out how to order it myself. I think I'm finally getting the hang of this online ordering stuff." By the depth of her dimples, I could tell she was proud of her accomplishments.

"That's great, Mom. But a Care Bear? Really? Couldn't find a normal adult costume, huh?" My lip curled involuntarily.

"Have you seen those adult costumes? My goodness. Do you think *this* is ridiculous? Can you imagine me as a naughty nurse or sexy bumblebee? Good-night! And besides, I like this one. It's my favorite Care Bear—Funshine. There's even a little sun on his belly. Look." She poked her stomach.

My mouth gaped as if there was only one word. "Wow."

"I bet the trick-or-treaters will love it! I can give them a Care Bear share with my belly." Pulling the hood over her head, she revealed fuzzy yellow ears. As if that weren't enough of a show, she went about situating her hands on her hips, shaking them to accentuate her belly.

Good grief. It has ears. "Jeez, Mother. Sometimes you're too much."

"I am no such thing. I'm just right. Just the way God created me. But, there might be a little bit of crazy mixed in from raising the three of you." She flashed me a wink then spun on her heel to walk away.

"Where do you think you're going?"

Without turning back, she replied. "This little bear has to go potty, and it may take me a bit to figure out how to get out of this costume." An insatiable giggle flitted in the air behind her.

As luck would have it, the sound of Lillian banging toys distracted me from my mother's wagging behind. "What are we going to do with Grandma?"

Lillian's mouth pulled into a toothless grin. My heart surged. It was hard to believe that I wondered if she came with a return policy only a few months ago. It is amazing what time and decreased postpartum hormones can do to improve a mother's bond with her child. Now her chubby, smiling face was enough to pull me to her. Leaning down, I placed my lips on the softest part of her cheek.

"I agree, baby girl. We'll keep her. She's pretty fun, huh?"

I placed another kiss on her nearly bald head and inhaled her baby scent. The mixture of powder and newness never got old. Each time I was near her, our bond strengthened like invisible chords weaving a tighter fabric.

"I love you, baby girl." Her chubby infant arms waved frantically as she cooed in reply. "Mommy better go get the candy before those kids arrive." Two steps toward the kitchen, I paused, sure I heard a faint voice.

"Sonya? . . . Sonya!"

"Mom, is that you?" I swung myself toward the bathroom, the last place she'd been. Now that I thought about it, she'd been in there a while. "Did you fall in?"

"No, I didn't fall in. I need help getting this costume off before I tinkle in my panties."

It was tempting to laugh until I sensed the panic in her voice. "OMG, Mother. Did you just say tinkle? And you know how I feel about the word panties."

"Fine," her voice still muffled through the door. "I'm going to pee in my underwear. However you want me to say it, you better get over here and help, or we'll have a mess to clean up. I got something stuck in my zipper, and I can't get it down."

Shaking my head, I jogged toward the bathroom. The green numbers that shone on the stove clock, 5:55, reminded me trick-or-treaters would be coming at any moment.

"Mom, we have to hurry. The kids will be here . . ." My words were cut short as I rounded the corner. Taking in the sight of the small bathroom, I lost all composure. My mother lay on the tile floor, squirming about while she frantically fought and argued with her zipper. Her shirt lodged in its teeth.

"Oh, my." My hands hit my knees as I bent over in hysterics. Spasms of laughter shook my body. "Mother, what in the world?"

"Sonya Joy. Quit your laughing, get over here, and help me. I'm stuck in here, and I really need to go—bad." The moment she completed her sentence, the doorbell rang in the background.

"Oh shoot. Trick-or-treaters. Hold on. I need to see if Joe can answer the door."

"Really?"

"Sorry, Mom. Just hold tight. I'll be right back."

I stuck my head out the bathroom door and shouted toward the stairs leading to the basement.

"Joe." My request elicited no response. I raised my voice an octave, "JOE!" Still no response.

Lillian, previously playing quietly in the other room, became frightened by my sudden yelling and began to wail with an intensity that rattled the windows.

Mom chimed in. "Oh, Lillian's crying. I'm so sorry. Let me get her."

"Mother, would you lay down so I can get you out." I leaned my head back out the door. "Lillian. You're okay, baby girl." Even my hushed, motherly tone couldn't calm her. *Where is my husband?*

Lillian continued to scream, her cry gaining intensity. "Mom, I have to go pick up Lil'. Can you hold it for a second more?"

The doorbell rang again. "Oh dang it. The trick-or-treaters."

"Yes, but hurry," she pleaded. "I'll keep trying to get unstuck."

I sprinted into the living room and scooped up my screaming infant, snuggling her tight, patting her back, as I hushed near her ear. "Where is the darn pacifier? When I don't want one, I find five. When I need one, none." I scanned the room, frantically searching for the precious paci. Locating one tucked near the couch, I hollered for Joe one last time before bolting to the front door.

As the door opened, a whoosh of cold October air assaulted my face. A cohort of ravaged children ambushed my candy bowl. Witches, princesses, tigers, and dinosaurs gathered around. "Trick-or-treat!" they yelled in unison. I threw handfuls of candy in each bucket as quickly as possible and briefly considered turning off the lights until the chaos inside subsided.

As the mob departed, my breath caught in my throat. For a moment and a reason I didn't fully understand, it was as if time stood still. The breeze that previously blew cold fall air calmed to a whisper. Standing in the glow of my porch light was a precious little girl. Her eyes, shimmering like stardust, locked into mine. *Why does it feel like we've met before?* She was barely three years old and wore an angel costume, whose glittery exterior reflected twinkling light onto my skin. She inched toward me, hesitant. Something about the way she clung to her mother's leg caught me off guard, misting my eyes. Stupid hormones.

"Twick-or-tweet," her high-pitched toddler voice was barely audible.

"Hi, sweetheart. Don't you look beautiful?" Still holding Lillian, I hunched down to her level, lifting the bowl upward. "Here you go, take as much candy as you want."

Seeing my baby, their eyes locked for the briefest moment. They reached for each other, their miniature hands connecting mid-air. They stayed that way, their fingers interlacing as if communicating something unspoken. A few moments later, Lillian cooed happily then looked back at me. Their connection broken, the mysterious child reached her delicate hand into the bowl, removing one piece before she turned to descend the stairs.

Compelled to say something, I blurted out. "Wait. What's your name?"

She tucked her head into her shoulder shyly before responding. "Towi."

"Tori." Her mother said, correcting her toddler talk. "Short for Victoria."

I gasped, unable to contain my surprise. "That's my mom's name," I said. The mist on my eyes joined together and trickled down my cheek. "Thank you for coming to visit tonight, Tori."

She nibbled her bottom lip briefly before separating them into a smile, and then she turned down toward the stairs. As I watched her disappear into the darkness, still mesmerized by our meeting, I squeezed Lillian, bringing her warmth close to me. "I love you, baby girl."

The cool breeze against my face broke my thoughts. Staring into the dark sky, blanketed with pinpoint stars, a flash of light caught crossed before me—the trail of a falling star. "Thank you for that."

"We better help Grandma out of her costume," I whispered to Lillian.

Seeing more festooned children coming my way, I knew there wasn't much time before the doorbell chimed again. I slammed the door shut and jetted toward the bathroom, nearly running over Joe.

"Where were you?" I blurted out. "I called for you twice."

"I'm sorry I didn't hear you. I was in the basement."

"It's okay. Sorry, I yelled. There's just a lot going on up here. Mom's stuck in her Care Bear costume. When I yelled for you, I scared Lillian, and she started screaming. Then fifteen kids arrived at the front door. It was a little crazy, to say the least. Then, the weirdest thing happened, but I'll have to tell you about it later." I was nearly out of breath retelling the story.

"Well, I'm here now. What can I do?" I pushed Lillian into his arms.

"Take her and answer the door if it rings. Throw some candy in buckets until I can get Mom fixed." Pressing a quick peck on his cheek, I whispered, "Thanks."

As I neared the bathroom, I heard Mom arguing behind the door. "You darn zipper. Ugh. Please help me, Jesus. In Jesus' name, open!"

"Ah-ha! I got it. Thank you, Jesus!"

Her celebratory giggle brought a smile to my face.

Still unaware I was perched outside the door, she yelled out, "Sunshine, I got it!"

"Ok, Mom, so proud. Did you pee your pants yet?"

"Almost, but I think I'm going to make it."

I breathed a sigh of relief in the aftermath of the craziness. With a chance to be still, my mind drifted back to the image of the little angel named Tori, who blessed my doorstep minutes earlier. "Mom, you'll never guess what I saw. A sweet little girl named Victoria in an angel costume. I can't explain it, but she had me so taken aback I started crying."

Even behind the door, I could sense the love in her tone. "That's so nice. So nice. Maybe she was an angel."

A warmth rushed over me, pumping through my body.

"Maybe she was."

March 2014

THE MOB

The trip had been planned for years—at least in my head. Only hours separated us from oceanfront beach chairs, all-you-can-eat buffets, sweaty cabana boys, and salsa dancing. Energy pulsed through my spine, electrifying my whole body.

"Do you need the list again?" It was the night before our departure, and I felt the need to make sure Mom was prepared.

"Nope. I'm all packed." Even through the phone, her enthusiasm paralleled mine. "I've got everything on the list—swimsuit, sandals, dress for restaurant, passport, ID, and gallon tub of sunscreen."

"Pretty sure I didn't write anything about a 'gallon tub.'" Even as I teased her, I realized her accuracy. We both understood the ramifications of a pale redhead who failed to apply adequate sunscreen—misery.

A few years earlier, my husband and I had traveled to a similar destination on our honeymoon. In the lazy haze of the hot sun, we spent an entire day poolside listening to the ocean crash while a polite Mexican gentleman brought us an endless supply of fruity mixed drinks. Though we'd remembered to apply sunscreen in the morning, between the lull of the waves, the warm sun, and the steady buzz, our reapplication was less than optimal. Our bodies were a patchwork of Mexican sunburn by the end of the day. We spent the entire next day hiding in the coolness of any shade we could find as heat discharged from our skin. Even today, the memory raised goosebumps on my skin. "On second thought, you bring the tub, and I'll bring the paint roller. I do *not* want to repeat my honeymoon experience."

"I packed SPF 100. I'm not taking any chances."

"Glad you're prepared. And since you're packed, let's go over the details." We poured through our itinerary from her arrival at my house that evening to the moment we'd step foot in the grand resort, our voices interjecting in our usual rhythm of excitement.

"I've never done anything like this in my whole life." She squealed so loudly into the phone that I jumped on the other end. "Growing up, I couldn't have imagined I would ever be on a trip like this. Thank you for making a dream come true."

I still knew little of her childhood. When the subject came up in conversation, she'd offer a few details before claiming she'd blocked out the details. In my heart, I knew there was more to her story. I would wait for the right time to ask her. Right then, I simply wanted to enjoy our experience.

"You're so welcome." As we talked, I stared out my living room window. The small grove of trees behind me waved at the mercy of the wind, their branches still bare in the spring coolness. "Mom, will you promise me one thing?"

"Of course, Sunshine. What is it?"

"Do you promise this time you won't get lost in the airport looking at palm trees?"

"I promise to keep my wandering to a minimum." She said remorsefully

"Don't be too hard on yourself, Mom. Your innocence is your best quality."

*****

Flying high above the white puff of clouds, I leaned my head on her shoulder and wrapped my hand around her arm. Her skin was different somehow, like it shimmered in the sunlight. As I focused on the tiny sparkle, she patted my arm with her other hand, a gesture I recognized as her silent "I love you."

By mid-afternoon, the wheels touched down in sunny Cancun, and we were giggling like two school girls. As we waited for others to depart the plane, I figured now would be a good time to warn her of the chaos about to ensue. Reaching for her face, I turned it toward mine. "Look. It's a whole new world down here, and I want to go through a few things with you. Okay?"

Her eyes became two wide orbs, white visible on all sides. She nodded.

Acknowledging her attention, I continued. "First, we have to get our bags. Can you try not to take out any sweet elderly people this time?" I joked, trying to lighten the mood.

A small puff of air escaped her lips as she crossed her arms in front of her chest. "That was an accident. I didn't realize the bags would come back around."

"I'm just kidding. But, in all seriousness, it's going to be crazy out there. After we get our bags, we have to take these forms we filled out to customs so they can make sure we aren't smuggling anything into the country." I tapped the immigration sheets she held in her hand. "You're not smuggling anything in, are you?"

She stared at me blankly, her face contorting in confusion. "What in the world would I be smuggling?"

"Oh, you know. Live animals, bugs, raw fruits, or any other kind of contraband." My comment only further solidified her confusion. "Mom, I'm joking. But seriously, don't smuggle anything in. You could get arrested." It took her a moment to process my comment. I watched as her expression shifted from confusion to clarity before I continued. "When we exit the airport, there will be gobs of people trying to sell us timeshares, cars, and such. You *have* to stay close. If you look like you don't know where you're going, they will eat you alive."

She stared at me wide-eyed, probably trying to decide how she could get the pilot to take her back home.

Noticing her nervousness, I rephrased my thought. "Okay, they probably won't eat you, but still, keep your eyes forward and don't engage in conversation. I know you. One smile from a stranger, and you'll be over at their desk handing them your credit card before you even know what happened. So remember—eyes forward, hold hands, smile, and walk fast. Got it?"

"Got it?" Her small figure looked up at me with innocence. Placing my arm around her shoulder, I squeezed. "It's going to be fun. Just make sure you follow me."

She nodded quickly as I felt her grasp my hand. "I've got you."

The plane was full, and it took quite a few minutes for us to unload. As I warned, the airport was a scene of controlled chaos. Travelers jimmied for positions in lines and weaved their way down packed hallways. I swiftly took Mom's hand, not allowing her an opportunity to get lost in the pandemonium. Her death grip squeezed me back. "Just remember, eyes forward and follow me." I gave her a reassuring grin and began to maneuver my way through the crowd—precious package in tow.

As we trekked through the airport, her hand still in mine, I could hear her behind me mumbling her own mantra, "Eyes forward, keep moving. Eyes forward, keep moving."

I giggled to myself, imagining what we must look like to other patrons—a grown daughter dragging her frightened mother through the airport as she mumbles to herself. *They probably think she has dementia.* The image made me laugh.

"What's so funny?"

"I was just wondering if people think you have dementia the way I'm dragging you through this airport."

"Sonya Joy!" She stopped dead in her tracks, jerking my hand.

"Oops. Too far? I'm just kidding. I'm sorry if I hurt your feelings."

She swatted my shoulder, and I placed my hand over it, feigning pain. She smiled wide.

We continued our venture as we moved through baggage claim and customs quite efficiently. I looked back often to ensure she was still following. As we neared the airport's exit, I stopped and pointed toward the double glass doors.

"This is where we walk past all those people trying to sell you things you don't need. Remember. Eyes forward, keep walking. Don't give anyone your credit card. You can say 'No, thank you,' but I generally just smile and shake my head. Once we reach the outside, it'll be hot, and there'll be many people waiting for taxis or buses. Stay close. Got it?"

Her nervous eyes danced around, overloaded with information. She finally locked in on mine and replied, "Got it."

She passed through the jungle of people like a seasoned champion—eyes forward, looking at no one in particular. When approached, she continued to shake her head and smile. I led the way, laughing at the scene. *God, I love this woman.*

As we reached the final doors, they parted, and the hot, humid air hit me like a wall. I stopped at the sight before me. Beyond the crowd of natives in brightly colored shirts and the blare of music from the margarita stand, the sun shone in radiant, intense beams on my skin. Long, thin palm branches waved frantically in a brisk wind. I took it in for a moment before the smell of exhaust filled my nostrils, the effect of the cars and buses lining the small circle drive. I turned to look at Mom.

In the splendor of the tropics, the mob around us seemed to disappear. Mom gently closed her eyes and graced my hand with a small squeeze. "I'm here, Sonya. I'm finally here."

"You sure are, Mom, and our fun has only just begun."

"Thank you, God, for this moment with my precious daughter," though she whispered, I still heard her prayer. "Thank you."

LET YOUR HAIR DOWN

A frequent visitor to Mexico, I'd witnessed these surroundings before. The contrast of grand, majestic hotel entrances against a background of dilapidated, broken homes and buildings was difficult for anyone to digest. Overwhelmed, Mom remained silent as her eyes scanned the scene. I felt her hand encircle mine as we rolled to a stop at a checkpoint where armed guards stood on their posts.

"It's okay, Mom. Those officers are a precaution. I've never had anything bad happen in all of my trips down here."

"Oh, I know nothing bad will happen. I'm just thinking." Her voice sounded small, like she was far away from me. The intense look on her face reiterated my feeling.

"About what?" Over the last few years, her thoughts had become infinitely more spiritual. Too often, I felt awestruck and somehow left out of a conversation I was not yet ready for.

"Just thinking about the people who live in some of these houses. It's easy for those of us born into a more reliable environment to forget the simple blessings. We take these gifts for granted when they become a part of our everyday life, but remembering to be grateful is one of the most pleasing gifts to God." Her gaze remained fixed out the van's tinted glass. "We're down here for the trip of a lifetime, to live in fun and excess, while some people have so little, and that's a reality we shouldn't forget."

I winced against her words, reminded of how often I glanced over my familiar surroundings, never pausing to realize the importance of what I'd been given. Even a cozy house in a safe neighborhood with plumbing and electricity was more than some people received in a lifetime. Rather than live in a state of gratitude, it was always easier to be frustrated with what I didn't have, or didn't like, than recognize what I did.

She turned to look at me reverently. "Maybe, I'll just pray for them on the way."

Her compassion was intense and occasionally caught me off guard. She was on a vacation that she had dreamed of for years, and rather than bubble with excitement, she turned her car ride into a prayer vigil for the less fortunate. As she gazed out the window, silently praying for those she encountered, I closed my eyes in gratitude for her example of compassion.

We reached our hotel shortly after our conversation. Waterfalls flowed from the massive concrete signs as lush tropical greenery rose from the highway. Mom's demeanor shifted from somber to awe, realizing this massive structure was the entrance. "Is this ours?"

I nodded quickly. "Wait until you see the resort."

"Oh . . . my . . . goodness." Each word pressed out in emphasis as she forced her nose against the window.

The driver checked in at the gate and then wound his way down the long treed drive. Anxious for the first glimpses of the resort, her head bobbed wildly toward each window. When the van rounded the last bend, the entrance came into view. Its large, magnificent exterior anchored by huge pillars and a massive water feature emerged from the forest of palm trees. She gasped. "It's beautiful. And huge! I've never seen anything like it. Are you sure this is where we are going to stay?"

The awe highlighting her face was infectious, and I embraced her spirit. "Sure is. Unless you'd rather stay somewhere a little less showy?" I smirked.

She rolled her eyes. "No way. This is incredible. I just can't believe it. And I can't wait to run down there and put my toes in the ocean." Her statements rushed out in rapid succession with hardly a breath in between.

I put up my hand to slow her down, "Breathe. I can't wait to put my feet in too. Can you just make me one promise?"

"Sure, sweetheart, what it is?"

"Can you *not* fall in the ocean this time? I really don't want to have to dry your skivvies in the bathroom again." Roars of laughter filled the van as we recalled the momentous occasion. Even the driver, obviously eavesdropping, began to snicker.

We were still laughing when the van slowed to a stop. The driver made his way around the vehicle and slid the door open. With a grand gesture of his arm, he declared, "Ladies, welcome to paradise."

The lobby, open to the outside in the front and rear, sported two square water pools with metal orb fountains in the center. The tile floor was polished to a mirrored shine. Toward the rear, the lobby was open to an expansive length of water-lined walkways. Vacationers meandered about, many sporting bright-colored drinks. The sun's rays peeked through as palm leaves waved in the distance. It was a tropical fantasy.

I'd been to this area before, but never this particular resort. Each visit to the Riviera Maya contained new anticipation and fervor to uncover all the resort had to offer. I closed my eyes, letting the salty air tickle my nose. Remembering my earlier conversation, I whispered in gratitude for the experience that lay before me. When I opened my eyes, I realized I could no longer see Mom. In her usual fashion, she'd become overwhelmed by her surroundings, and tears trickled down her cheeks.

"Hola, *Señoras.*" The driver's words interrupted our silence. Shaking her head as if to awaken from a dream, Mom turned to look where the voice was coming from.

"Excuse me," she asked.

"Sorry to interrupt, *Señoras*. Your bags are unloaded. They are by this pillar, safe with Juan until you check-in."

I slipped a few dollars in his hand before heading toward the front desk. "*Gracias*, sir."

"*Gracias, Señora,*" he nodded, then made his way back to the van.

The front desk was stately. Dark wooden panels anchored the massive slab of granite covering the surface. Mom, standing on her tiptoes, could barely see over the edge. She attempted to converse with the hostess behind the desk despite her height disadvantage.

"What are you laughing about?" She stared at me, confused.

"I think you're getting shorter with age." She waved her hand, dismissed my comment, and went back to find the attention of the front desk attendant.

"Excuse me? Holler."

I twisted instantly and watched as she waved the poor woman down. Mortified, I covered my face, shading my eyes. Grabbing her waving hand, I pushed it to the counter.

"Mother, what are you doing? Haven't you ever checked into a hotel? You have to wait. And did you just say 'Holler?'"

"Yes. Isn't that how you say 'Hello' in Spanish?"

I attempted to whisper, but disbelief began to take over. "It's *Hola*. Like oh-la, not ha-ler. That's a slang word for 'Hello.'"

"Oh shoot." She slapped her forehead. "I knew that didn't sound right."

"It's okay. I'm sorry if I sounded upset. I was . . . just surprised. You have to be careful when speaking another language. If you say the wrong word, it might mean something offensive. How about you stand right here," I shifted her shoulders, facing away from the desk, and kissed her forehead. "You can look around at the scenery, and I'll get us checked in?"

"Yeah," embarrassment still evident in her tone, "It's probably best."

"Don't be sad. You were trying to fit in—which is commendable. I don't know much Spanish either. Hello, goodbye and wine are about all I know." I hoped my joke would improve her mood. "Maybe give yourself a few days and try again."

"I think I'll go wander around the lobby while you get us check-in." Her previously sunken shoulders straightened as her tone perked a little.

"Ok, but don't go too far. I don't want you to get lost."

"I promise to stay close." She held her right hand high as if being sworn into a courtroom, then turned on her foot and headed off.

The lobby was expansive, with two sidewalks leading toward the ocean on both ends. I peered forward, noticing a small seating area just a few yards from where we stood. Vacationers emerged, umbrellaed drinks in hand. "It looks like there is a little bar just down the walkway. If you want, you could go order something fruity. Tell them you want a Piña Colada." I wondered if she would take me up on my suggestion, given her preference to abstain from alcohol.

"You know, I think I might. I'm on vacation, after all."

"That a girl." I raised my hand to give her a high five. "I'll meet you there. Behave." Her hand connected with mine.

"I always behave." Her eyes twinkled.

"I know Mom, but this is a foreign country, and you are on vacation. You gotta let your hair down. At least a little."

"Okay. Maybe a little." She raised her thumb and index fingers, spacing them closer together. As she walked away, she turned back to smile, giving her hair a little flick.

"That's right, Mom. You can finally let your hair down. I hope you have the time of your life."

EMBELLISHMENTS

"Having a little trouble there, Mom?"

It had only been a few minutes since checking in, but Mom was well on her way to the end of a piña colada. Juan, the bellman, was showing us to our room, and even though she swore the glass she held in her hand was her only one, her limited tolerance was already showing its effects. She swerved slightly as we walked. Distracted by her surroundings, she ignored my question.

Juan and I chatted as best we could with the language barrier.

"Bird!" Out of nowhere, Mom shouted louder than I'd heard her shout before.

"What in the world?" Confused about her outburst, I whipped my body around so fast I nearly lost my footing.

"Look, it's a bird." She declared; happily, her words slurred.

"Yes, Mother. We have those in Iowa." She ignored my comment. Years of being ribbed by her family members made her immune to our comments.

"I know we have birds, but not *this* kind." She pointed to a small painted bunting perched in a low set palm tree.

"I'm giving you a hard time. I remember being equally excited about the change in scenery my first time here. I guess I just wasn't expecting it to be so loud."

She rolled her eyes. "God is such a talented artist. Don't you think?"

"Talented indeed." Large weaved palms shaded our walk along verdant grass-lined sidewalks. Perfectly manicured lawns were spotted with African tulips and shaving brush trees blooming in the sunshine. Low set palm trees completed the perfect tropical backdrop.

As Juan led us down the terracotta tiled hallways, I caught the first sounds of the ocean. The majestic, meditative crash of the waves against the shore lulled against my senses. I closed my eyes for a moment, matching my breath to its rhythm.

"Sonya, I hear the ocean!"

Sensing Mom's excitement, Juan piped up. "Ah, yes, ma'am. We will, ah . . . see it soon."

"Oh, oh, oh. I'm so excited." Her semi-altered state appeared to evaporate as she stood straight, furiously scanning the horizon for her first glimpse of the vast blue water. "There," she pointed straight ahead. "There it is. Can we go to it?"

The ocean, to her as well as me, had become a beacon of peace.

"Soon." A smile anchored my face—her excitement infectious. "Let's drop off our bags and let Juan help some other guests. Then we can go."

She looked over to Juan. "Oh, I'm so sorry. I forgot you probably have more guests to help. And here I am blabbering on about birds and palm trees. I just can't wait to sit in a beach chair and feel the sun on my face."

Juan smiled, his teeth bright against his mahogany skin. Dark chocolate eyes sparkled as he took in the joy Mom radiated. She had a history of making an impression. "Oh. It is no problem, *Señora*. Our landscape *es* very *bonita*."

"Bonita?" Mom asked, lips pursed in confusion.

"Ah. Sorry, Ma'am. *Bonita* is beautiful in English." He bowed his head slightly, embarrassed by his mistake.

Mom noticed the self-conscious way his eyes cast downward and patted him on the back. "No worries, Juan. You're right. It is very *bonita*." Her touch immediately relaxed him.

The sound of the ocean's cadence continued to increase as we approached the door to our room. We continued down a long hallway, rooms lining both sides. Bright Mexican colors of red, yellow, and aqua accented the walls spotted by dark brown doors. Since it was Mom's first experience with an all-inclusive tropical resort, we splurged for an ocean view room. Juan slowed as we reached the door. He pulled the key cards from his shirt pocket, inserting it into the carved wooden door. As the door swung open, bright white sheets gleaned against dark mahogany headboards. Thick, lush pillows abounded on each bed with a signature towel swan nestled among the plush bedding.

We shuffled forward, entranced by the ocean's pull. Sheer curtains billowed in the breeze, revealing tall glass doors. We reached them simultaneously, pulling the curtains back.

Mom gasped. "Look, Sunshine. It's like the gates of Heaven opened wide."

"Stunning, isn't it? The heartbeat of God—setting the cadence for the rest of the world."

Still staring into the vastness she murmured, "I don't know what a cadence is, but it sounds beautiful."

Her thin pink lips curved at the edge, extending toward her eyes that creased at the sides—the pure joy in her expression connected with a portion of my heart, expanding within my chest. *Goodness, I've missed her.*

With our attention fixed on the water, she began to speak in quiet reverence. "You're right, you know. I can feel God's heartbeat in the rhythm of the ocean. But He isn't just a part of the sea; He is part of you," though she paused, her eyes never shifted. "He is within your heartbeat, your breath, and your soul. You are never alone in this world. Don't forget that. He is always with you—I am always with you." Finally, releasing her stare from the window, she looked into me. The intensity within her eyes called to me. Whatever she was about to say, I was meant to internalize. "Time, space, death—nothing can keep us apart. You'll understand now that you have Lillian. As a mother, your child is a part of you, an invisible cord that can never be broken."

I knew in my soul everything she declared was the truth. When I held my child, I recognized it was a bond no force could ever break. Just as I was tied to Lillian, I was equally bonded to my mother—an unbreakable force forged by our Creator.

"A bond never broken." I wrapped her close to me, watching as the ocean disappeared into the horizon. Though I could no longer see the water beyond the line where the sky and sea met, I knew it still existed. Similar was the bond between a mother and daughter or myself and God. I nestled a moment with my thoughts before I wiped the wetness from my cheeks.

"Enough of this sappy stuff," I sniffed. "Let's get out there and soak up some sun before it's too late."

Giving me a squeeze, she tucked her head into my shoulder. "Good idea. I'm going to get changed. I've got some new beach accessories I can't wait to show you."

I raised my eyebrows, eyes wide. With my mother, I was never sure what I was about to encounter. "What kind of accessories?"

"It's a surprise," a sneaky grin crossed her face.

"It's not a thong, is it?"

"Sonya Joy!" She turned to me, mouth agape. "Why in the world would I wear a thong? No one would want to see that. Goodness. I'm just talking about a few embellishments. Geesh."

I shrugged. "It was a legitimate question. You never know what you might see on these beaches. There are people from all different cultures here. So be prepared."

Her hands gripped her hips in seriousness. "I will not now, nor will I ever, be sporting a thong." She shook her head at the notion of herself in the revealing attire.

"Just had to check." I smiled. "In that case, I can't wait.'"

*****

Thirty minutes later, we were ready for the beach. Mom sported a floral swimsuit with a flowy skirt, a wide floppy brimmed hat, and sunglasses too big for her face. "Oh. Aaaah. . . . Well." I struggled to hide my amusement as I took it all in. "Did you get a new hat?"

"Sure did. The man at the store told me these were in nowadays and I needed a pair of these fancy sunglasses, too. How do I look?"

I forced my lips together, struggling to hold back laughter. In reality, she looked completely overdone and touristy. Still, no opinion of mine was worth wiping the smile off her priceless face.

"You look amazing." I struck a quick pose, hand on hip, and tilted my head into the air. "Completely ready for a grand beach vacation. Should we go soak up some sun?"

"Of course," she squealed.

Loaded like pack mules, we hauled our overflowing bags toward the beach. Since most of our day was spent traveling, we arrived after the usual beach crowd. We easily found two open seats adjacent to the shore. After unloading our bags, we fluffed bright beach towels onto the chairs.

Spraying on a quick layer of sunscreen, I fell into my seat, finally allowing my eyelids to drift closed. The push and pull of the sea massaged away the tension in my tight muscles. I inhaled deeply, allowing the salty breeze to intoxicate my nose. Though late in the day, the sun was warm and gentle against my skin.

Lulled by the rhythm, my mind began to wander, as it often did. I thought again of her words earlier, ". . . time, space, death—nothing can keep us apart. As a mother, your child is part of you, an invisible cord that can never be broken.' She was right, of course. It didn't matter what the circumstance, the memories and the love we shared, meant we never had to live apart. With her by my side, the thought comforted me until a loud snore broke my peace.

Poor lady must be exhausted from our travels. I glanced around, trying to see if anyone had noticed her, but with the setting sun cast a golden glow over the great expanse of water, only a few sun seekers remained on the beach.

Feeling the nip of the breeze, I tapped her shoulder.

Despite my gentleness, she awoke with a start. "Ha? What?" Her hand flung to her face knocking her glasses crooked, dislodging her hat from her head.

"It's okay, Mom. You were just sleeping. It's starting to cool off. We should probably go back and get ready to eat."

She wiped the drool from the corner of her mouth and glanced around to see if anyone noticed. "Oh goodness. I was tired."

"Traveling can zap your energy."

"Sure did." Feeling the breeze on her skin, she shivered as tiny bumps covered her arms. "I suppose we should get back. It's getting a bit nipply out here," she crossed her arms, covering her bosom.

I looked at her, confused. "You mean *nippy?*"

"Huh. I always thought it was nipply because of well . . ." She looked down, scanning her front. "You know."

"Oh goodness, Mother. Seriously? It is most definitely *nippy,* not *nipply.* Where do you come up with these phrases?"

She shrugged deeply. "I don't know. I guess I just misunderstand what people say. But it makes sense, doesn't it? *Nipply?*"

"I suppose, but either way, we better head back inside," I said, exasperated.

Lifting herself from the chair, she began to pack up her bag but paused briefly, crossing her hands in a simple prayer position before she mouthed, "Thank you."

Her act of gratitude stirred within me. I shuffled toward her, jockeying for position among the bags and towels she carried. Linking my arm in hers, I sent my own silent "thank you."

Lost in thought as we ventured back, I couldn't help but remember all the years I'd crawled up onto her lap and dreamt about a vacation like this; precious time spent with the woman who loved and molded me into who I'd become.

"Look, Sonya. Butterflies."

Shaking my head to clear it back to reality, I noticed the roost dancing on a gust of wind. "Beautiful," I said, squeezing her arm, "simply beautiful."

THE PAST

"**W**hat do you think?" I asked as Mom devoured the last of her dessert. "It was all so interesting," she said, her mouth still full of food. "I would never have put some of those combinations together, but it was delicious."

We were seated in one of the reservation-only restaurants on the resort. The atmosphere was modern. The low, dim lighting was underscored with bright multi-colored lights strategically placed along the wall. Angular seating and decor embellished the small space—nothing like the cafe-style restaurants back home. Dinner was a new experience, three courses of savory fusion paired with wine. Timid at first, with her limited culinary background, she eventually grew fond of the intriguing combinations like watermelon sage soup, chocolate pumpkin salmon, and a chili fudge brownie.

"I don't know. You got pretty creative with food combinations when we were growing up. Not everyone mixes cottage cheese and strawberry Jell-O or pudding with sandwich cookies." I winked.

"Oh, hush." She swished her hand, waving off my comment. "I know my cooking wasn't anything special, but that easy approach was all I ever learned. I traveled between homes so much when I was young, I never really mastered cooking." Her voice trailed off, retreating to a distant memory. Disappointment hung heavy on her face, diminishing the sparkle usually present in her eyes.

With my thumb, I traced tiny circles around her hand. "Hey, I was only joking. I hope I didn't hurt your feelings. It must have been difficult being transferred around as a child."

Born to a single teenage mother, she never met her biological father. When the subject of her past arose, she'd quickly claim her memories were fuzzy. She'd briefly refer to living with her grandparents or aunt and uncle a lot, always speaking highly of them. Beyond those details, it was as if she never wanted to recall, let alone share, any details.

"It was . . . hard." Her voice trailed off as she recalled another time. Her eyes glazed over as if she were in a different world entirely. I leaned in, leaning my head in my hand, knowing this was a rare moment. "There was always a disconnect between my step-father and me. I wasn't his, and he wasn't mine, and we couldn't seem to reconcile that barrier. But I had a lot of people who loved me, and Elvis to keep me company." She grinned self-consciously, bringing the light back into her eyes. "I spent hours in my room imagining the day he would drive down the lane to my house, pick me up and take me to Graceland." Her giggle released the seriousness previously tied to her face. "Oh, Elvis." She placed her hand on her heart, mocking a swooned teenager.

I sensed she wanted to change the subject, and though I longed to respect her privacy, there was a part of me that needed to delve deeper into the past she rarely told of. I spoke gently as if talking to a frightened child. "What was it like growing up? You don't really talk about it."

"For good reason. To be honest, so many memories during that period are very fuzzy. The atmosphere at home was," Her mind trailed off, distracted by another blurred memory, "difficult. It was better for everyone when I stayed with my grandparents." She stared across the restaurant, noticing a family at a nearby table. The parents, probably in their mid-thirties, tended to their two small children who giggled furiously about something. Though laughing themselves, the parents attempted to shush them. Mom's face was a mixture of amusement and longing, witnessing a childhood she had never experienced.

She looked back at me. "But, there is one thing I can say. Even as a little girl, I always knew God existed. My grandparents took me to church. And as I sat in the padded pew and inhaled the deep scent of wood and flowers, there was always a warmth, physical and internal, within those four walls that wrapped me in overwhelming love. I never understood where I belonged at home, but I always had a place there, with God. It was as if a protective barrier formed around my body at church so no heartbreak could bust through. It would try and occasionally succeed in knocking a small chip off here or there, but when I prayed, I could feel God rebuilding my fortress."

She paused for a moment and closed her eyes. Though I couldn't be sure, there was something about the slight grin on her face that had me certain she was imagining just such a time. I could see her, a child of five or six, light red hair barely visible over the pew, sitting quietly in the large expansive space as she allowed the love of God to wrap around her thin frame. A child snuggling into the arms of her Father.

She blinked her eyes open, trying to focus in the dimly-lit restaurant. When our eyes locked, her apple cheeks rose with her smile.

"I always knew, no matter what came at me, no matter how difficult or heart-wrenching, God would always be my strength. I have tried to share that love with you and your brother and sister, but I failed sometimes." Teardrops formed in her eyes as her lip began to quiver. Her voice, though sure in its words, began to shake.

"I'm so sorry for the times I wasn't everything you needed. But I hope you always know I loved you all so very much." She dabbed her eyes with her napkin.

My heart broke. How could this woman, who had shown me such indelible love, ever feel she was deficient? Just like every good mother, there were times she was stern, but I never, in all my years, wanted or needed for love. "I know, Mom, and we love you too. No mother . . ."

Her head, held down ashamed of her past, glowed in the candlelight at the table.

I gave her hand a pulsed squeeze. "Hey, look at me."

Slowly, she raised her head. Her eyes, red-rimmed and wet, met mine across the table. "No mother can be everything for her children. We aren't meant to be. We are only human. That's where God comes in, just like you said. He fills in the gaps and crevices of our human weakness. Well, God, and Elvis, of course.

"You've been an undeniable example of love, kindness, generosity, and faith to so many. We, your friends, family, even strangers you've met only briefly, are so blessed to have known you. Never feel bad about who you are or how you got there. Your love, like God's, is my cornerstone—something I never doubt. I'm more sure of your love than I am of anything else. I know, no matter what I do or say, your love will never cease in its consistency. You are a true reflection of God's love. It's a biblical love, and you should be proud."

She stared blankly, lost in her own memories of hardship, as tears dotted her cheeks.

"Mom. Did you hear me?"

She looked at me with an intensity I'd never seen before, a seriousness I almost didn't recognize, like she was in another place. "Oh, Sunshine. I may have been a little distracted, but I heard every word. Knowing you felt my love the way it was intended fills my heart with so much joy. There are many parts of my life that I am not proud of, and I back away from. But you, your siblings, and our family—you are the best decisions I ever made. You all make up for any hardship I encountered when I was younger. I hope you all never forget how much I love you."

Her words, honest and powerful, had us both blubbering muddles. A mess of mascara stained our cheeks, highlighting our red eyes and puffy faces. I stood from my chair across the table and scooched in next to her. Placing my arms around her, I hugged her with every ounce of love I carried in my heart. I willed my love to fill any empty space within her soul. "We love you, Mom. Your past, present, and future. We love you in your emptiness and fullness, your darkness or light. We love you."

She buried her head into my shoulder. I leaned into her and uttered a silent prayer. *Dear God, thank you for her beautiful blessing of love, so constant and consistently mirroring yours. Fill her mind with memories of us, our family, and the love we share. Erase any of the hurt and hardship from her past. Help her to know, undoubtedly, her perfect example of your love.* As I whispered the final words, I felt her body begin to relax, releasing the tension of the past she harbored so deeply within. "You are so loved," I said.

We embraced a few moments longer before her head finally lifted. We brushed the tears from our eyes and smiled gently. "I guess we shouldn't discuss such heavy topics when we've had so much wine." Grinning, I wiped one last tear from her cheek.

"I guess not." A small smile hinted at the edge of her thin lips as she blew her nose.

"Thank you, Sunshine. For this trip, for your friendship, for your love. Thank you."

"Not time, space, or even death could separate my love from you, Mom." I kissed the top of her head one last time before standing.

"Think we've had enough excitement for one day? Want to stroll through the resort on the way back to the room?"

I offered my hand to help her up and linked my arm into hers. We meandered slowly back to our room, mesmerized by the pulse of the ocean and the twinkle of the lighted pathways. Gratitude filled my heart as I walked, joined to the one who knew me first, whose heartbeat once lulled me to sleep. Without her, there was no me.

GLIMPSE OF HEAVEN

"**O**h goodness, Mother, what are you doing?"

"I'm going over there." She pointed to a small poolside area crowded by teenagers in scantily clad bikinis. Loud music blared in the background while a hunky Hispanic twenty-something explained the upcoming Zumba lesson.

After our emotional dinner conversation and late-night stroll through the resort, we both slept soundlessly, soothed by the ocean. A renewed energy surged, leaving us amped for the day's adventures. Mom's newfound zest had motivated her to partake in the dance fest about to ensue.

"Are you sure you want to do that? There's going to be a lot of teenagers shaking their booties," I leaned toward her ear, "and other body parts."

One lid half squinting in the sun, she set her eyes squarely on mine. "You better believe it." With wide, raised arms, she twirled around. Then, giving her bottom, donned in a navy striped swimsuit, a little shake, she whispered, "I've got some moves of my own."

My mouth hung open in pure shock. Fully aware of her newfound vigor, the thought of my sixty-something mother gyrating with a group of millennials stunned me.

"Are you going to come too?" She asked, curling a pointed index finger toward her as she backed away.

"Absolutely not!" I wrinkled my face in disgust. "I haven't had enough to drink to embarrass myself like that. Besides, dancing in my bikini with total strangers is not really my idea of entertainment."

"Oh yes, you are." She snatched my hand before I could pull it away and began dragging me toward the blaring music. Though I knew I could fight her off if I really wanted to, a small part of me longed to concede to her more carefree lifestyle.

As we neared the dance area, I noticed a few brave older vacationers scattered amongst abundant teenagers. We packed into the concrete walkway while the instructor, Antonio, explained the routine. As she watched Antonio gyrating in his too-tight T-shirt and short shorts, her face was priceless.

As Antonio began to shimmy in rehearsed positions, Mom tried to follow his lead. Unaware of her incoordination and oblivious to staring onlookers, she danced to the beat of her tune. While her eyes were closed and distracted by the music blaring from the speaker, I crept away from the mob of dancers. While I didn't want to be among the group, I watched from the side in admiration of her free spirit, unbothered by the judgment of others.

When she finally turned and noticed I wasn't there, she searched the crowd. Finding me off to the side, she flashed a wide grin and quick wave before returning to her dance.

After about ten minutes, the music began to die down. Looking at the crowd of dancers once again, I caught a glimpse of Mom giving Antonio a quick high five and a one-armed side hug. Her personality was infectious, and even strangers were drawn to her. After a quick thanks to Antonio, she shimmied back to where I stood.

"Did you have fun?"

She was out of breath; her hands propped on her knees. "Oh goodness, yes." With pursed lips, she shimmied her hips. "That Antonio sure knows how to move."

"Oh, I'm sure he does" I tapped her nose playfully. "Another one of your brothers, I assume?"

"Ha! Absolutely—though we might not share the same dad, with that skin tone and all." I listened as she laughed freely, no longer chained down by the weight of the world.

"Mother. You're ridiculous. If I didn't already know, I'd ask what's gotten into you." I swung my other arm around, completed my hug, and then quickly pulled away. "And sweaty. Ridiculous and sweaty. Are you ready to sit and lounge by the beach again, or do you need a shower?"

"Very funny." I watched her nose wrinkle as she felt her own damp skin. "The beach sounds great, but now that you mention it, I think I'll rinse off first. Then we better slap on some more SPF 200. I can feel my skin getting a little crispy."

"SPF 200, huh? That sounds serious."

"Well, if there is one thing we redheads are serious about, it's sunscreen."

I looked at her, getting lost in the irony of us here as the wind blew pieces of her red hair across her face, the sun reflecting off each strand. As a child, I dreamed of warm, tropical vacations with Mom. When she got sick, I thought my dreams would die with her diagnosis. Little did I know that the bond of a mother and child is woven so tightly, that no circumstance could take these moments away—even if they weren't exactly how I'd envisioned them.

Moved by the moment, I kissed her sweaty forehead. "Okay, let's go rinse off, lube up, and then we can sit and relax for a while."

*****

Minutes later, we were back in our beach chairs, stroked by the warm ocean breeze. The wind carried the sound of rustling palm trees and seagulls searching for food. Children splashed and squealed at the shoreline while waves crashed, creating a foam border on the sand.

I was eager to finish reading a book I'd started a few weeks ago, but with work and a little one at home, time was limited. Digging it from my bag, I sat back to read.

"What book you got there?" Mom asked.

I flipped the cover so she could see it. "Proof of Heaven. It's about a neuro-surgeon who didn't believe in God until he had a near-death experience. It's quite interesting."

"Does it describe what heaven is like?"

"I haven't gotten that far, but it's part of why books like this intrigue me."

She sat forward in her chair, swinging her legs around to my side, removing her fancy glasses so that I could see her eyes. The truth settled between us. "Heaven is perfect. I'd say it's not so much a place as a state of being. We don't need a physical location for our souls. Heaven is the true position of being one with our Creator. It's pure and light—freedom from pain, hurt, fear or anger. No negativity, just joy." She blinked her eyes, releasing mine, and rested her head back, her lids closing. Previously hidden by a large cloud, the sun pierced through an opening and beamed directly on her freckled face. "The smile of a child or the hug of a loved one, a magnificent sunset or the sound of this ocean, feelings of joy, generosity, gratitude, and love—that's heaven."

Her image of heaven settled over me like a blanket on a cold day, soothing the chill. "That's a stunning description, Mom. You definitely have a strong opinion about heaven."

"I guess you could say it's like home."

"So you're saying it's not all cherubs and harps?"

She grinned, returning her glasses to her face, "Definitely not *all* cherubs and harps."

"Wouldn't it be nice if we could all find a little heaven on Earth?" A seagull jutted from the sky, piercing the water before ascending into the sky, a fish in its beak.

It was a moment before she spoke, and I wondered what she was thinking. When her words finally broke the silence, her tone was reverent. "When you find God as your true source, trusting Him for all your needs, you spend less time striving and more time trusting in His plan. That's when you find a bit of heaven here on Earth. But the rest," she inhaled deeply, "the rest is worth waiting for."

Relaxing my head against my chair, I placed the book in my lap. My eyes shifted from the pure turquoise of the ocean to the white sand below. The sun created a ripple of brilliant light across the ocean surface.

She was right. Of course, heaven wasn't all cherubs and angels. Heaven was a state of being one with God, one with the pure love of our Creator. There were days I felt I couldn't wait until it was my chance to go to my heavenly home, to fully be connected to the ones who had gone before me, but there was far too much left for me to do here.

KEEP THE JOY

"You got it?" I reached a hand to help heave Mom's suitcase into the overhead bin.

"Good grief. They do not make these racks for short people." With one final push, her baggage found its final resting place. She let out a sigh. "Phew. That was more than I've worked out all week." The back of her hand wiped her brow. "Well, except that dance with Antonio." She shimmied, a mischievous look on her face.

Nearly the last to board, we quickly took our seats as the flight attendant's voice buzzed over the intercom. Following a quick seat belt check and safety instruction, it was only moments before the aircraft pushed back toward the runway.

My mind drifted into a fond childhood memory. Growing up, I was deathly afraid of thunderstorms. The bright flash of light across the sky followed by the loud crash of thunder was enough to bring me instantly out of my bed and next to hers. The double bed my parents slept in was too small for me to share, so I'd find my spot on the floor, sleeping bag in hand, and nestle in as close to the frame as possible. She'd sense me laying there and drape her hand over the edge of the bed, lacing her fingers into mine. Any fear the thunderstorm caused was quieted by her hand in mine.

As the plane sped up, her hand gripped mine and released me from my memory. Sensing her nervousness, I reached my other hand over to enclose hers. We remained quiet for most of the flight home. The stillness was a pleasant retreat, as my body felt equal parts relaxed and exhausted from our time in paradise. We had shared such intricate and intimate details of our lives over the last few days. I couldn't help but picture her as a small child, sitting, hands folded in the pew of a giant church with the silhouette of Jesus sitting next to her, his arm wrapped around her fragile shoulders, as a protective father would. I couldn't fathom what it must have been like, and my heart ached for the child, the innocent one who longed for a complete sense of love and belonging.

My chest ached again as I thought that even for a moment, she'd wondered if she had done enough for us. Her silly, naive, loving self was always enough, and I prayed she would know that to the depth I did.

Looking at her now, eyes closed, resting with such serenity, as if she were in another place entirely, I nestled my head against her shoulder, her hair tickling my face. Sensing my closeness, she turned toward me. She placed a gentle kiss on my forehead. Her touch, at that moment, more than any before felt spiritual. Lightness filled my being, like a wave of peace entering my soul.

"I love you, Mom. So much. I wish we could see each other more, but for now, I'm grateful for the time we have."

"I love you too, Sunshine. I know God has such beautiful, prosperous plans for us both. It's not always easy to see the wonder of His intention when we're standing in the darkness. But if you trust Him, listen for Him in the silence of your heart and move forward in faith, He will reveal the glorious unfolding in due time. Keep the faith, keep the joy and follow His ways. You *will* be rewarded."

Head still rested on her shoulder. I shut my eyes. Feeling the remnants of emotional exhaustion filter my veins, I surrendered to the exhaustion. "Keep the faith, keep the joy," were the last words I recalled before drifting into a soundless sleep.

January 2015

SOMETHING IS WRONG

"I just feel like something is wrong, Mom. I can't explain it. There are no real signs or symptoms, but I can't shake the sense something isn't right."

I was halfway through the pregnancy of my second child and had told only those closest to me, Joe and Mom, about the unrelenting feeling something was wrong with the baby.

Earlier in the week, we'd gone to our twenty-week prenatal ultrasound. Fear nagged at my mind, the way a muscle spasm refuses to release. I stared anxiously at the large screen near the ceiling as the ultrasound tech squeezed more goop on my belly. Though my medical degree gave me enough background to recognize some of the pixelated black and white images, I was no expert in prenatal care. I hung on her every word but caught no hint of surprise or concern as she went along.

"Everything looks okay?" I asked as she pushed the probe against my lower abdomen, apologizing intermittently for the pressure.

"I can't diagnose anything directly. That's for the doctor to do. But, unofficially, I don't see anything concerning." A quick scan of her facial expressions found no cause for worry.

I couldn't believe what I was hearing. I'd convinced myself something was wrong in the last few weeks and was certain the doctor would give me a diagnosis to coincide with my concern. But to my great surprise, the test was completely normal. Minutes after the last bit of blue gel was wiped from my abdomen, the tech led us to a nearby exam room. The doctor, a thirty-something with curly blonde hair that draped onto her green scrubs, marched into my exam room, propping herself against the sink. "Everything looks good with the baby. Lungs, heart, bones, everything. Any other questions?"

A flash of heat crossed my forehead. Of course, I had questions. If everything was good why was I still plagued by a sense that something wasn't? Despite my concern, I couldn't bring myself to ask her. After all, she'd just confirmed everything looked fine. She'd probably tell me it was normal for women to experience worry during pregnancy and blame it all on the hormones. I didn't need someone else telling me I was overreacting, tired, or, worse yet, hormonal.

Laying back onto the exam table, my mind continued to flurry as the doctor measured my abdomen. In silence, I wished her words would release my fear.

Pushing the stirrups back into the bed, she scribbled some numbers on my chart. "If you have nothing else," she paused, and I swallowed hard, forcing back the words on my tongue. "We'll see you next month." Handing me a check-out sheet, she exited through the door.

Hearing the door close, I yanked my coat from the hook and pulled it on quickly. I grabbed for Joe's hand. Obviously unaware of the torment in my mind, he went on excitedly about it being another girl, making sure I knew he wasn't the least bit disappointed it wasn't a boy. The cold Iowa wind bit my cheek as we stepped out the door, and I lifted my fur hood over my head. Not wanting to talk, I bid him a quick, "I love you," kissed his cheek, and faked a smile before stepping into the shelter of my own car.

*****

Still feeling anxious and not ready to be alone with my own thoughts, I called Mom. My thoughts spewed out as soon as I heard the ringtone stop. "I know the doctor says everything is fine, but I just can't shake this feeling something isn't right. It probably is just my hormones and the pain getting to me. Or, maybe I'm crazy. I don't know." One hand on the steering wheel, I reached the other to massage the constant ache on the right side of my back. For weeks I'd dealt with an unrelenting spasm. With treatment options limited due to pregnancy, I was forced to endure the continuous sharpness that had taken up residence along my spine.

It was a long moment before she spoke. I glanced at my phone, thinking the call had dropped like it often did on this stretch of highway, but before I could say "Hello," she spoke.

"Sunshine, you aren't crazy. I'm sure the pain is getting to you, but you should never ignore a mother's intuition. I'm not saying there will be anything wrong, but you must pay attention to your gut feelings. God places those nudges on our hearts for a reason. I don't know what He's trying to tell you, but right now, the most important thing you can do is pray. Sometimes all we can do is hand our uncertainties over and have faith that though the answers aren't clear right now, they will be someday."

A flutter rolled through my abdomen, and a smile tugged at the edge of my lips before a tear reached my sleeve, the wetness expanding. I prayed every day I was wrong, that my feeling was more of a misguided sign of exhaustion than of intuition. But, even through my prayer, the thought lingered.

Staring into the road as it stretched before me, darkness descended with the last remnants of the sun dipping below the horizon behind me. "That's easy for you to say. I've got this precious little baby inside me, and instead of being excited about her arrival, I'm terrified. And the worst part is, I can't fully express why."

"I know, Sunshine. Believe me. It isn't easy for me to say. I saw a lot of heart-ache in my life, but it's only with time and my closeness to God I've been able to feel confident in His plan."

Each beam of the oncoming headlights raced past me on the highway. The lulling consistency with which they passed somehow calmed my frayed nerves, and I was grateful for the sensation.

"Did you find out what you're having?" Mom's question jarred me back to reality. I knew she was asking about the baby's gender, but her question was a perfect outlet to lighten my sour mood.

"A human, Mom. We're having a human." I said, matter-of-fact.

"Sonya Joy!"

And there it is.

"You know what I meant." The high resonance of her voice with her signature huff triggered an inadvertent giggle. The chronic tension from my shoulders began to release.

"Looks like it's a family of girls for us. Poor Joe." Though many women often prayed for one of each gender, I was thrilled to be having another girl. Nothing against boys, but having two sweet girls, with all the ribbons and curls, felt right to me.

"A baby girl." Her voice was soft, reverent even. "I *knew* it. It's all granddaughters for me." And she wasn't kidding. With my older sister having only two girls and my brother one, it truly was a family of granddaughters for her.

"You knew it, huh? You could have fooled me. That second pillow you made has blue fabric. Seemed a little boyish to me." Before I'd even decided to have children, my mother made pillows for all of her grandchildren—a sweatshop project. Hidden on each one was a smudgy inked fingerprint from their Grandma Vicki. Not wanting to leave me out, she pre-made two pillows for my, yet unthought-of, children. One was brightly colored with pink speckled ladybugs, the other, red and navy with Noah and his ark.

"Ah, but perhaps you failed to recognize the importance of the fabric lies deeper than the color. Do you remember Noah's story? His ark is a sign of the covenant, a promise of safety for your faithfulness in following God's commandments. Maybe your intuition is right. Perhaps there will be something unexpected when your baby girl is born, but no matter what may come, you can believe that God will guide you through."

I shivered at the thought, glanced down, and whispered to my unborn child, "You think Grandma's right? Everything's going to be okay? Mommy doesn't know what will happen sweet girl. But there is one thing I can tell you—I'll do whatever it takes to keep you safe."

I was never one of the women who leaped for joy when they realized they were pregnant, though I never mentioned that feeling to anyone. In fact, if I was honest, both times I felt guilty. It seemed so easy for us to conceive when I was always so unsure of myself in the beginning.

"What did you say, sweetheart? I didn't hear you?"

"Nothing, Mom." I shook my head, clearing my thoughts and recalling the pillow we were discussing again. "Thanks for bringing a little clarity to the situation. I never knew you were such a biblical scholar," a tinge of sarcasm in my voice.

"There isn't anything scholarly about me. I have just been spending a lot of time with Jesus lately. Kinda opens your eyes, you know. Well, and your mouth, I guess." She snorted through the line.

Once again, I felt my face relax into a smile. "I love you."

"Love you too, Sunshine. Take care of those girls."

"Always and forever."

"Always and forever," she repeated as I heard the click ending our conversation. In the light of the glowing dashboard, my baby girl was just beginning to expand my waistline.

"I'm not sure what's to come, Lord. But I do know, there's nothing we can't get through with you by my side."

June 2016

NOT MY PLAN

I couldn't wait for it all to be over—the constant boring pain in my back, the restless nights, and the unrelenting feeling that there was something wrong with my unborn baby. I was over being pregnant and ready to meet my little girl. I was in the throes of an emotional hissy fit when Mom called a little too early one morning a few weeks before I was due.

"Good morning, Sunshine. How are you?"

"Not so well, Mom. I'm still feeling miserable. I guess pregnancy isn't as exciting to me as it is for some people."

"Still worried?"

My days had been filled with constant prayers for the life growing within me. Thinking about the apprehension I couldn't shake, my throat tightened.

With three-year-old Lillian still asleep upstairs, Joe was spending a quiet moment alone in our bedroom, and my sister, down for a visit, still in the basement, I found a rare morning to myself. As often happened when I was alone, I allowed my thoughts to wander too far. Placing my coffee cup into the dishwasher, I crossed to the window, noticing the gentle breeze ripple the lake's surface.

"Yes." I felt my eyes betray my fortitude as pricks of wetness gathered in my eyes, blurring my sight into a watercolor of blue and green. "Call it intuition or crazy. I just can't shake the feeling."

"Sunshine. You've been under so much pressure lately. You work too much and can't sleep. I wish I could take it all away from you."

"I know you would, Mom. You've always said you would take away any heartache or pain we endured," my voice trailed off as it began to shake.

"And I always meant it. I just wanted you three to be happy."

Despite our distance, I could still imagine the reverence and love that shaped her face. I pictured the way the light caught her blue eyes, and her lips pulled across her teeth. "You've always been one of the best parts of my life, Mom. And I know this baby will be, too. Whatever may come, I know God will be at our side." In my mind, it was no longer if something was to come, but what. Closing my eyes, I mouthed a silent prayer.

> *Heavenly Father. I know you have plans for the sweet innocent life within me. I know you knitted her and created her just as she is meant to be. My heart wants to ask for a healthy baby, one I can hold and snuggle from the moment she's placed on my chest. My soul longs for the beautiful, loving experience so many are blessed with, yet I've never gotten it. I can't release the feeling this will not be the case, no matter how deeply I wish it were. So today, Father, my prayer is that you will promise to be at my side and keep us both safe whatever may come.*

"Sunshine? Are you still there?"

"Huh?" I blinked, releasing the tears that hung from the edges before pulling my attention back to the phone. "Sorry, Mom. I got distracted for a bit. Did you say something?"

"I was just saying it will be good for you to go to church today. Your sister said she was coming down to watch Lillian while you and Joe go to mass together. It'll be nice for you to have a little undistracted God time."

"Yes, it most certainly will." I scanned my watch. "Speaking of which, we better get going, or we'll be late."

"Okay, sweetheart. Try to rest in God's plan today. Love you."

"Love you too, Mom."

*****

Twenty minutes later, Joe and I were sitting comfortably in the second pew of our old Catholic church as the cantor sang. I loved our church. The way the old wooden pews creaked when I sat and the smell of incense in the background. The candle burning near the tabernacle reminded me of the precious gift protected behind its doors. Smiles from fellow parishioners we met over the years greeted our arrival. There is a warmth that always surrounds me there. It felt like home.

Finally able to attend fully to the mass, without the distraction of playing air traffic control for the tyrannical demands of a three-year-old, I embraced the quiet and bowed my head in silence. For months, my every prayer sounded alike. "Lord, why do I feel this way? Father, please release my worry and give me a healthy baby." But today, in the peace of His house, surrounded by signs of love and sacrifice, my prayer felt reformed.

"Lord, I'm not sure what the next few weeks will bring. Only you know the fate of my beautiful unborn. Today Lord, I ask only for peace. The peace that comes in knowing You will always be there for us and, together, we can get through anything."

I listened as the lectors read the word of God and the priest shared a moving homily. New life rose within the church that day and I was abuzz with hope. I hooked my arm into the crook of Joe's elbow. His hand, much bigger and warmer than mine, further relaxed my anxiety. Though still uncertain about the coming weeks and what difficulty they may hold, the uninterrupted God time was exactly what I needed.

As the pianist strummed her last chord, we slowly filed out. In my periphery, I noticed a waving hand. The bony fingers belonged to a petite woman in her late sixties with short greying hair. Not recognizing her, I assumed her wave was meant for someone behind me.

Near the back of the church, the woman continued her frantic wave in my direction. Her eyes locked with mine. Pushing against the parishioners to reach me, she grabbed for my hand and pulled me into the adjacent pew. Confused and slightly concerned, I followed her.

"Excuse me?" Her voice was confident despite her much shorter stature. "You're probably wondering why I brought you over here." With eyes so dark her pupil nearly disappeared, she stared into mine, and I nodded in agreement. "I saw you two up there." She pointed toward the pew we recently left. "Even from back here, I could tell how much love there is between the two of you." She glanced down to my belly, as most did, given my newly found status of huge. "When you stood, I realized you were expecting. And fairly soon as it looks."

She was spritely, and I was intrigued with what might have moved her to accost a total stranger, not to mention the slightly offensive comment. I began to doubt her sanity.

Before I could interject my thoughts out loud, she started again, speaking faster than I expected. "It's so heartwarming to see young couples, such as yourselves, praying and sharing in God's love."

I politely smiled though I remained confused. "Thank you. That's very nice of you to say."

Thinking our conversation had come to an end, I shifted my weight, ready to exit. My retreat was halted before I could meet the end of the pew. "Well, anyway, I should get to my point."

"Thank goodness." I thought. "This is getting awkward."

Her face tightened with a seriousness I hadn't yet noticed. Her eyes, vivid in intensity, seemed to pierce into my soul. "I called you over here to tell you something. You've been praying for something for a while, haven't you?"

The familiar lump rose in my throat, my mouth too dry to swallow. My hand instinctively reached my swollen belly, heavy with the life that thrived within. *How could she know?* Confused and stunned, my response was only a whisper. "Yes."

"I thought so. While you were praying up there, God told me to tell you something. I guess He chose me because He knew I wouldn't be afraid to approach you." Her cold hand touched mine, and I resisted the urge to pull away.

"God wants you to know, whatever you are praying for, it's going to be ok. It's going to be His plan, *not* your plan, but it's going to be all right." Her hand gripped mine as she stared further into me. "Does that make sense?"

Shock pulsed through me, but the clarity of what she spoke was instant. She spoke of my baby girl, the precious life I'd carried for nine months. I nodded silently as her form blurred behind my wall of tears. "Thank you." The words hardly escaped my parched lips.

Attuned to my fragile emotional state, she released my hand. "You're welcome. I hope it helps."

I clutched Joe's hand and bolted from the pew. *How could she know? God, did you really tell her to say those things? And if so, why wouldn't you just tell me?*

Thoughts raced through my mind as I rushed to the safety of my car. Hitting the button to unlock the door, I swung it open and fell into the seat, slamming the door shut. I lost all composure. A flood of emotions rushed through me. Shock transfused with relief that I wasn't crazy, that the nagging sense of uncertainty was real. The shock merged into gratitude for a loving God who could see my emotional suffering and choose to bless me with this incredible gift.

There in the security of my car, I allowed myself to succumb to the rush of emotions bottled within me. I sobbed. Each heave of my lungs released pent-up worry and pain. Tears fell from me like rain, splashing against the steering wheel.

Joe sat motionless next to me, knowing I needed a moment to comprehend what had happened. His fingers touched my arm. When my breathing began to slow, I turned my swollen eyes toward him.

"I knew I wasn't crazy. You know what I've been praying for every single day for the last nine months." I rested my hand near my unborn child. I could feel her gentle movements intensify with time. A tiny bulge stretched out to meet mine as if communicating the new truth.

I pressed my finger against the pressure. "Mommy doesn't know what's to come, little one, but you heard what she said. You're going to be okay. Not our plan—God's plan. I love you, little angel."

I stretched for my seatbelt and clicked it in place. Shifting the car into gear, I backed slowly out of the parking lot. I drove in silence. Though my body made no physical sound, my mind was chaotic with endless chatter. I ached to remain in the peace of knowing God had blessed me with an incredible gift, but the questions were too intense to be silenced. *What's wrong with my baby? Will she have some sort of disease? Will it be permanent? What does 'okay' mean?*

The disquietude within me all these months was more than the hormonal imbalance of a pregnant woman. It was gracious God mercifully preparing me for whatever was to come.

As we reached our house, I pushed the shifter to park, and glanced at Joe. Still unable to fully comprehend the magnitude of what had transpired, I reached for him. Not needing an explanation, he nodded. The bond between my mother and I was so tightly woven that he knew I would need to talk to her.

He pushed open his car door then turned back to me, "I love you. Come find me when you are done talking to her." He blew me a kiss then exited, shutting it softly as he retreated toward the house.

I anxiously waited for her to answer before my recount of the events shot out like a rocket. I told her the entire story. The feelings rushed back as I explained every detail. Overwhelmed, once again, my tears returned. "Mom? What do you do with a blessing that is most certainly going to contain heartbreak?"

After a short silence, her soft voice filled my ears. "Oh, Sunshine. What a beautiful gift He has bestowed upon you. I'm sure it comes with the heaviness of uncertainty, but you must not forget His plan is always better than ours."

"I know you're right. My head is just reeling. Why wouldn't He have just told me? Why would He use a stranger?" I rested my cheek against the coolness of the window, my tears fogging the glass.

"Sweetheart, I'm sure He did tell you numerous times. I'm sure you read it in a verse, or one of those books you're always reading. You may have heard it in a homily or the words of a friend. But, like most of us, when we are looking for a specific answer we desire so deeply, we often miss the actual one. That's why your feeling persisted. It kept you praying every day for your baby. Seeing your faithfulness and love, He bestowed on you a precious gift—a direct answer to your question. Not necessarily the healthy baby you were praying for but instead His answer. Now it's time for you to rest. Rest in His love, knowing, just as He said, everything is going to be all right."

My head swirled, dizzy from the chaos of emotion that stirred within me.

"Easier said than done."

"I know. But you have been blessed with so much. A loving husband. A precious daughter. A new life to carry. Rest in those blessings. Now, go let that wonderful husband of yours hold you tight and know that it will all work out just God planned."

"I'll try. I love you, Mom."

"Love you, too."

I rested my head back on the headrest and pressed my eyes tight. Heaviness covered me, further decreasing my ability to breathe. I sat silently for a moment, trying to catch my breath before opening the door. Ascending the stairs to the house, I was glad my sister had taken Lillian to the park. I needed to find Joe. Finding him, I fell into him, tucking my head into his neck, smelling his familiar fragrance and the feeling of security it released. With what little energy I had left, I whispered. "I don't know what it means, but I know you and God will be with us no matter what."

His deep voice reverberated in my ear, "No matter what."

Inhaling once more, I leaned closer. "Okay, God. Your plan, not mine."

WHATEVER IS TO COME

"Lord, I know this is supposed to be Your plan, and I respect that notion. But hear me out. I'm so exhausted. Hours of standing have overwhelmed my battered body. I can't sleep or get comfortable. I realize something unexpected is to come, but I know Your peace, which surpasses my understanding, will comfort me. With You, I am ready to face what's to come, but I need her to arrive—like now."

Thirty-nine weeks, five days pregnant, and I was miserable. Lying in bed, I stared through the darkness, fixated on the ceiling. I had reached a stage of pre-delivery desperation. The weight of the unknown bore deeply into my heart. It was one o'clock in the morning, and I had resorted to pleading.

I heaved my rotund belly and flipped to my side, vying for a comfortable position—the mere shift an act of extreme effort.

Snuggling into my pillow, I listened to Joe's steady breath, jealous of how easily he slept. Just as the soft, steady rhythm of his respirations began to lull me to sleep, a swift kick to the bladder jolted me awake.

"Really?" I whispered loudly to the peanut nested within. "Now you kick me? Not five or ten minutes ago, when I was already awake?"

I shifted to my back and flailed my legs rapidly, attempting to gain the momentum necessary to heave myself off the bed. After several convincing groans, I finally succeeded. After a quick fist pump to celebrate my success, I waddled to the bathroom. Reaching the cool tile floor, a rush of warm liquid hit my leg.

"Holy Moses, my water just broke."

A moment of disbelief passed before I grabbed a towel to wipe my leg then waddled back into the bedroom. "Joe," I whispered, not wanting to startle him.

The edge of sleep still in his voice, "Yeah?"

"My water just broke."

Dazed from the early morning wake up, he replied, "Huh?"

"I said, my water just broke. We have to get going."

Finally recognizing the magnitude of my statement, he jolted out of bed. "Okay. Okay." He scanned the room. "What do you need me to do?"

I rolled my eyes. *You would think this is the first time.*

"While I call someone to watch Lillian, why don't you get the car packed?"

"On it." He darted toward the bathroom to gather a few things before heading back to get the suitcase and quilt. He glanced toward me, lifting the precious cloth above his head. I nodded in approval as he slipped out the bedroom door.

*****

Forty-five minutes later, we were checked into the maternity center and only minutes more before reaching my room. The nurse, kind and gentle in her work, swiftly strapped me to a concoction of wires and monitors. "I'll get the IV in so we can start some antibiotics. Then I'll leave you to get some rest. Any contractions yet?"

"No." I frowned. With my medical background, I was keenly aware the risk of infection increased with time from when your water broke to delivery.

"You're going to start Pitocin, aren't you?" I cringed. I despised Pitocin—an IV medication often given to increase the strength and amount of contractions. But increased strength meant increased pain, and the pain was what I was afraid of.

"I'll have to confirm with the doctor, but it's likely." She smiled sympathetically.

"I just hope my epidural works this time." I knew the odds were not in my favor that this one would perform any better than the previous, and her expression confirmed my suspicion.

"Anything I can do before I leave?"

"No. Thanks."

She gave my IV one last look before disappearing behind the large door.

I glanced at Joe seated in the corner, eyes closed, head rested against the wall. Despite his awkward position, he emanated peace. He was always more confident in his faith and serene amid uncertainty. Seeing him, I was reminded how blessed I was. Even our love story was one of trusting in God's infinite plan.

As if sensing my gaze, he slowly opened his eyes and curled his mouth into its familiar smile.

"I think I'm going to talk to Mom before I rest a little." He nodded in understanding.

*****

"Hello?" Her voice was more awake than it should be at the early hour, and I wondered if she was waiting for me to call.

"Hey, Mom. I just wanted you to know my water broke."

"Sunshine. That's wonderful. You've been praying for that."

"Yeah, I was actually praying for it two minutes before it happened. We're at the hospital now. They have me all hooked up to the monitors. All signs point to stable for me and little girl."

"But you still can't shake the feeling?" She must have sensed the apprehension in my voice.

"No. It's rooted too deeply, I suppose."

"It can be difficult to let go of fear. But instead of choosing fear, wrap yourself up in the warmth of God's peace. Snuggle into it like a blanket on a cold night. Let it sink into every part of you. And remember, everything is going to be okay. He told you so himself."

I paused for a moment and closed my eyes, focused on relaxing my muscles, allowing peace to replace tension. My personality tended toward control rather than calm, and surrendering my fear would be an arduous task.

"Sunshine?"

"I'm still here. I was practicing peace." I couldn't help but smile.

"Oh, good. I thought I had lost you. You have the blanket with you?"

"Of course. I wouldn't have this baby without it."

"Snuggle into it. Feel the love and prayers of everyone who can't be there physically. Sense the peace of God in its weight. Then rest, Sunshine. You may have a long road ahead of you, but know, at least for a little while, you can rest."

I felt the fabric between my fingers and the love that seemed to release as I weaved my way through the quilted cloth. "Rest sounds good, Mom." I felt the heavy pull of my eyelids as I fought to keep them open.

"I'll see you soon."

At her declaration, I finally closed my eyes, feeling her presence surround me. "Mom?"

"Yes, Sunshine."

"I just need you to know how much I love you."

"I love you, too."

Settling into my bed, nestled beneath the weight of the quilt, I inhaled deeply. Each inhale, tranquility. Each exhale, releasing fear. Allowing my tired eyelids to collapse finally, I snuggled in deeper. "Ok, Mom, I'll rest now. I'm ready for what's to come."

PITOCIN

An intense clenching pain clawed at my abdomen, waking me. I clasped my hand to the pain until the sharpness began to subside. As it eased, I looked over at the IV pole near my bed and recognized a new medication bag hanging from the steel hook. The clear, deceptively trivial liquid dripped slowly from the chamber connected to the tube inserted in my hand.

"Pitocin." I spat the word.

In a haze of exhaustion, I vaguely recalled the scene that had transpired earlier. A nurse had placed a soft hand on my shoulder so as not to startle me, "Any contractions yet?"

Still half asleep, I shook my head no and allowed my eyes to close again, weighted by fatigue.

"If they haven't started, the doctor wants to begin a medication to help move things along." Before she'd even finished, I'd fallen back to sleep. I thought it was a dream.

But now awake and feeling the pang of another pull, I drug myself further from sleep. As the wave passed, I scanned the room for the clock—4:30 a.m. I'd been asleep for almost two hours.

I peered in the corner and noticed Joe beginning to stir. "Did the nurse say anything to you when she was here?" I asked.

"No. Why?"

"Oh, nothing big." My breath caught as another upsurge of pain rolled through me. "Whoa. Those are getting stronger." I took a moment to allow the pain to stop before I continued. "As I was saying, she started a medication to increase my contractions. I thought I was dreaming when she told me. Did she mention anything to you?"

He rose from his spot on a small couch in the corner of the room and started toward me. "Nope. I've been asleep over there." He smiled remorsefully.

"Don't worry about it. I wouldn't expect you to stay up the whole time. You need rest too. I think I'd better call the nurse and let her know I want an epidural, though. If I wait too long, I might miss my window."

The golden rays of the June morning reflected in the sky as the anesthesiologist knocked politely on my door. Working with them frequently, I welcomed the familiar face. She proceeded swiftly. I heard the snap as she donned her gloves and listened for the familiar crinkle of the packaging as she opened the sterile container. I breathed through the intense tightening of each contraction, trying hard not to think about the six-inch-long needle about to be inserted in my spine. Sometimes, I wish I were oblivious to it all. The pain eased as the numbing medication flowed, and I no longer cared about the logistics.

I turned to look at her. "Thank you so much. I'm praying this epidural will be more successful than my last."

"It went in well, so it should. But if it doesn't, or anything changes, please make sure you have them call. My shift is ending, so it'll be someone else, but we want you to be comfortable." Her sentiment was genuine.

"I will. Thanks again."

"Anytime." She gathered her remaining garbage into a ball and placed them neatly in the trash before heading toward the door. "Hey, and good luck." With a final wave, she left the room.

Though the reprieve of the epidural had been nearly instant, it became clear within fifteen minutes it was no longer working. Each contraction began to intensify as tears drew to the edge of my eyes with each compression, deepened by the power of Pitocin. Joe stood beside me, and I squeezed his hand, hoping to release some of the burden. *Please God, not again. I cannot go through this pain again.*

I rang for my nurse, who appeared within moments. With each claw of pain, I cried loudly. "I can't do this. You have to call them back up here. This epidural isn't working. Please." I knew I was probably being unreasonable. I knew plenty of women who had children naturally and survived, but I didn't want to be one of them. For months I had suffered the deep emotional pain of believing something was wrong with my baby, and I was not going to endure the physical suffering, too.

"Please." I choked between sobs. "You have to turn down that medication."

With every bit of calm and gentleness in her voice, she asked, "Do you want me to stay with you? I can help you breathe through some of them. If we turn down the Pitocin, it might delay your progression. You're dilating well."

"No. I can't. I'm sorry I'm such a wimp. I just can't. Please, turn it down and call the anesthesiologist back. They know me. Tell them my name. Please." She must have heard the hysteria in my voice as she dropped the rate of the IV. The contractions began to dull minutely as she retreated from the room.

"Joe." My voice was defeated. "I can't do it again. It's worse this time. The contractions hurt more than last time.

"I know, Love. She went to call the doctor. I'm sure they'll fix it."

Without prompting, he placed his face beside my ear. I listened as his familiar voice began to pray to the only one who could fix this all. "Dear God. I know this entire plan is yours, not ours. I just ask that you would help the doctors to give Sonya some relief from her pain. She has already endured so much through this pregnancy. If it is your will, Lord, ease her suffering in your great mercy. In your son Jesus' name. Amen."

I breathed deeply, inhaling his fragrance. Over the years, the refreshing, masculine scent had drawn feelings of security and peace. I clutched his arm as another contraction took hold. When the pain released, I heard a knock at the door.

"Sunshine?"

"Mom!" I wept at the sound of her familiar voice. It never ceased to amaze me. No matter how old I became, there were days I just needed my mom. I wrapped her into a swift embrace as she neared the bed. Snuggling into her softness, I clung to her.

Still sobbing, I began to explain, "Mom. It hurts so much. They started this medication, and it's making it worse. They gave me an epidural, but it's not working. Now I can't move my legs, but I can still feel the pain. I know it's not their fault, this is how the last one was, but I can't go through this again, Mom. I just can't. Please make it go away. Please."

She smoothed my hair back with her hand and gazed at me with softness in her eyes. At that moment, I allowed myself to feel like the scared child I was, no longer the adult who had to endure it all. "Sweetheart. It's going to be okay. You will get through this delivery. Take a deep breath." She inhaled long and deep, and I followed. I pulled her closer as the wave of another contraction rolled through my body. When it released, I heard another knock at the door.

"Hello? Can I come in?" I heard the familiar deep voice from behind the door.

"Come in." I wiped the tears from my eyes, trying to pull myself together.

As the doctor approached, I shook his large hand and met his eyes. "Thank you for coming up here. I'm sorry I'm such a mess. Do you think you could fix this?" I pointed to my back. "It doesn't appear to be working right. At least I hope this isn't as good as it gets?" Despite my pain, I attempted a laugh.

"Well, let's see what we can do. I've been putting these in for a lot of years. I've got a few tricks that might work."

After discussing the options, we removed my non-working epidural and placed a new one lower than the first. "Over the years, I've found some people have slightly different anatomy, and this has been successful."

"That sounds like me, 'slightly different.'" My laugh halted in my throat at the start of another contraction.

He worked silently behind me. Though I faintly detected the needle poke, I felt my entire lower body relax in one swift movement when the medication began to flow.

"Better?"

I exhaled in relief. "Yes, thank you."

Feeling the pain alleviated, I whispered. "Thank you, Lord."

Looking up at the nurse, I pointed to the bag of Pitocin hanging from the pole. "Turn it up if you need to. I won't be moving from this spot until I have to. I'm in good hands now."

She smiled as she reached to increase the dose. The machine beeped loudly.

I thanked the doctor once more before he exited, then gently positioned myself back into the bed and snuggled in. "Wake me up when you need to recheck me."

"Just rest for now. I'll be back later."

I looked at the clock. Six-thirty a.m. Almost two hours.

As the nurse left the room, I looked gratefully from Mom to Joe, then closed my eyes into another rest.

THE ARRIVAL

The doctor arrived, her youthful face calm and eyes bright. "She definitely wasn't on the night shift. This is good. I got a fresh one." I thought, understanding the nuances of a doctor at the end of a shift. Her mind will be clearer than that of a doctor who spent the entire night delivering babies.

"Sorry to wake you." Her voice was cheery for the early hour. "How are you doing?"

"Amazing. Let me tell you. This whole labor thing is an entirely different animal with a working epidural. I can't feel anything but a little pressure." I scrunched my nose, drawing in a breath, slightly embarrassed, "Though, I'm fairly certain I haven't moved my body at all in over an hour. Not even an inch. I was afraid if I did, the pain might return."

She grinned politely, understanding the implication. "Well, I think it's time we do another check. Which means you will have to move at least a little." She winked before making her way to the side of the room. Grabbing two gloves, she snapped them on her small hands.

I shimmied down, sloth-like, willing nothing to dislodge. After a quick check of my unmentionables, the doctor's face appeared above the sheets.

"Nine centimeters and one hundred percent effaced. You're almost there." Tossing her gloves in the trash, she placed her hands on her small hips. Something about her stance drew attention to her youth. I was confident she was younger than me. Her girlish glow and chipper personality eluded she was not yet jaded by years of long hours and burnout. Her height was limited, perhaps barely five feet—*the perfect height for catching babies.* I giggled to myself, excited to have my spunk back.

"What?" she asked, perplexed by my laugh.

"Nothing." I shook my head. "Probably just delirious. Apparently, my babies only want to start this action in the middle of the night." Our light laughter filled the room in unison.

"Most do." She rolled her eyes quickly, probably all the sleepless nights she'd endured already in her young career.

"Well. We have a couple of options here. Because you are getting so close, you can try to start pushing. Or, since the baby is stable and you're so comfortable, I can give you more time to labor down on your own before we start."

I stared at her, befuddled. My knowledge of baby delivery was limited despite my medical background, especially considering all I could remember about my first labor experience was *OUCH!*

Seeing my confusion, she continued. "Labor down means letting your natural labor, or contractions, bring the baby further down into the birth canal without you pushing as much. Unless you have a good, working epidural, most women don't choose this route."

"Thank you for the clarification. I choose that. Let's labor down." I peered sneakily at Joe. "I feel like I'm playing Let's Make a Deal, and I just chose door number two."

Joe rolled his eyes while Mom burst out laughing. "Sonya Joy." She shrieked, shaking her head.

The doctor snickered. "Okay. Door number two it is. I'll be back in a little bit to check on you. If you need something before then, just push your call light."

I gave her a silent thumbs-up. *Man, epidurals make me spunky. This is the way to do it.*

As the doctor departed, Joe glanced at me, drawing the sweet smile I'd loved for years across his face. "You're in a much better state than you were last time."

"Tell me about it. I don't think I'll ever have another baby, but if I do, I'm choosing door number two."

He closed his eyes and shook his head. Usually the grounded one, he moved his chair closer to me. "Do you want to read the daily readings while we wait?"

We'd become accustomed to reading the Bible verses sent out each day by the church. I was amazed how often the words would strike deeply into my soul as if they were written just for me.

Retrieving his phone, he made quick work of finding the readings. A man's voice, thick with an Irish accent, recited the first verse. "A reading from the book of Isaiah Chapter, 'Listen to me, you islands; hear this you distant nations: Before I was born the Lord called me, from my mother's womb, he has spoken my name.'"

As the word womb crossed my ears, I shifted toward Joe. He rose a silent finger to his pursed lips. "Shhh, let's hear the rest." I could feel the tears begin to curtain my eyes. Mom, in the corner, appeared as a blurred image like stained glass on a church window.

The reader's strong voice continued, "I have labored in vain; I have spent my strength for nothing at all. Yet what is due me is in the Lord's hand, and my reward is with my God."

"Joe." My voice was nearly a whisper. The implication of the verse was not lost on our weary bodies. "God's speaking to us, again."

His hand tickled my skin as his fingers wove into mine. He turned toward me, our unspoken words an acknowledgment of the weariness.

"I know, Love. I know." He wiped a stray tear from the apex of my cheek. "Should we listen some more?"

I nodded.

The lector continued. "A reading from the book of Psalms. 'For you created my inmost being; you knit me together in my mother's womb... I praise You because I am fearfully and wonderfully made; your works are wonderful, I know that full well. My frame was not hidden from You when I was made in the secret place, when I was woven together in the depths of the earth.'"

My tears collected, then drifted downward, leaving a trail of wetness on my cheek. My mother, a hand over her mouth, wept in the corner.

"Oh, Sunshine. Listen to His words. She is wonderfully made. Knit together in your womb, perfectly the way He planned. He's reminding you no matter what is to come, it's in His forever perfect plan. What a gracious God we serve."

I clutched my abdomen, feeling the squeeze of the muscle below. I breathed into the contraction's pull, relieved the pain was still abated. The time was near.

Soon I would meet my precious baby, and we would begin our adventure together—whatever that might hold. Closing my eyes tight, I spoke internally to God.

"The road has been long, plagued with pain and fear. But through it all, you've remained continuous in your grace. I don't know what's to come. But I'm sure, in my humanness, I will fail to recall your generosity, and for that, I am deeply sorry. Please keep us wrapped in the safety of your strong, gentle arms. Protect us from fear and doubt that will, no doubt, come upon us. Make clear our path, Lord, so we may live in accordance with your will. Help us to remember that we are following your plan. She is fearfully and wonderfully made. Knit together just as you would have her. In all our ways, Lord, let us acknowledge you. In Jesus' name, Amen."

Silence engulfed the room, all of us lost in thoughts and prayers for the innocent life about to enter the world. The pressure in my abdomen increased in preparation for delivery. It wouldn't be long now before I met my precious baby.

As if on cue, the doctor arrived. Noticing our tear-stained faces, she asked, "Did your pain return?"

"No. Just a lot of pressure. I think it's time."

Donning gloves once more, she checked my progress. After a short time and a lot of pressure, she stood. "You're all set."

She turned toward the nurses behind her. With the precision of a pit crew, she was dressed in gown, gloves, and mask within seconds.

The pushing commenced. I couldn't shake the nagging feeling of what was coming even through the pain. What was our plight? Would I hold my baby this time, or would she be rushed away like Lillian? The struggle of mental and physical exertion raged within.

Joe and Mom took their positions on each side of me. With each push, I attempted to release some of the worries I felt tugging on my soul. Three giant pushes later, and she was released.

Her cry was instant, a beautiful sign of life and breath. "It's a girl." The doctor smiled widely, highlighting her youthful face. "Do you have a name?"

"Sophia Eleanor." Joe and I said in unison.

"Well, sweet Sophia, here's your mommy." The doctor made quick work of swaddling her before laying her on me. Her delicate face was swollen and pink.

Her eyes were closed and goopy with the ointment the nurses had placed there. I began to sob, big, heavy, happy tears as I held my newborn baby.

After the commotion of the delivery quieted, I stared at her round, swollen face, and my fears sat in. I listened intently to her cries and knew there was something wrong. Her wails were not the steady wails of a newborn; each breath was followed by a quick, short gasp as if she were trying to swallow air.

"Excuse me?" The nurse, still nearby, turned her head when I spoke. "Does her breathing sound normal to you?"

She listened intently, though it was easy to hear. "Sometimes, newborns make a noise if they've inhaled a little gunk on the way out. The more she cries, the more it should clear out. If it doesn't get better in a couple of minutes, we'll take her down to the nursery and get a closer look."

No matter how deeply I wanted to believe her, I couldn't. My entire pregnancy led to this moment. Like the culmination of the play's first act ending with a cliffhanger to the next scene. I knew, deep within my soul, this was not my "happily ever after." At least not yet.

Her breathing continued steady but labored like a fish out of water. My intuition rose within me, and I bristled against it. I wanted so intensely the beautiful newborn experience so many others had. I longed for the gentle, endless cuddles and soft squeaky baby noises. But even stronger than my desire for normalcy was my longing for safety, for healing.

I stared into her precious grey eyes, still glassy with ointment. "Hey, my sweet angel. Momma really wants to keep holding you right here, but the doctors need to look at you a little closer. Okay?" I felt a tightening in my chest as tears welled. "Daddy is going to go with you, but just as soon as I can, I'll be there too. You and I are in this together, little one." I kissed her soft cheek, inhaling her scent. I placed the memory deep in my soul to carry with me in the days to come.

As the nurse gently removed her from my arms, a chill remained where her warmth had been. "I love you, Sophia. Momma will be with you soon, baby."

I gazed helplessly as a piece of me walked out the door again. Shrill sobs filled my lungs. "Mom, I know this is God's plan. But why does it have to hurt so much?" Placing my head into her shoulder, I released all the anguish bottled within.

"Oh, Sunshine, I don't have all the answers. I know it hurts, but we just have to trust. I'll be right here by your side." She patted the quilt still lying on my bed, "Me and everyone else who loves you. We'll always be right here."

Swollen and broken, I looked toward heaven. "I know you said your plan and not mine. Be with my sweet baby. Please don't take her away. I've already lost so much in this life. Please keep her safe. Help me to rest in your love and in your plan."

Though I tried to fight it, exhaustion took over my body. Within moments, as I drifted into sleep, I uttered once more. "Momma loves you, Sophia."

SWEET SOPHIA

woke in a panic, disoriented. In the absence of my epidural, my body ached. Instinctually, my hand shot toward my abdomen. Where it once held life, it was now barren. The recollection of the previous hours flooded back, "Sophia." Fear choked me.

Frantically, I scanned the room, desperate to find my baby. I prayed her absence was a dream consciousness would erase as the four walls shrank around me. Gone was the safe, clean feeling of the hospital I'd grown to love, and in its place, isolation from my baby.

"Hello? Anyone?" I scanned the room for a clock. "How long had I been asleep?" Within moments of my desperate cry, Mom appeared in the corner, as if I'd glazed over her presence in my stupor.

"I'm right here, Sunshine." Her face came into view. A blush of sleep flushed her cheeks. When she reached me, her hand tenderly brushed a stray hair from my face.

"Where's Sophia, Mom?" Sensing my nervousness, she reached for me.

"She's in the nursery. She's stable, but her breathing is still labored, so they're doing some tests."

A familiar squeeze continued up my throat, quickening my breath. I knew what stable meant—safe, secure, steady. But years in medicine had taught me that distinction could change any minute. Labored and stable didn't belong together. Their opposition did not go unnoticed.

Even though I'd prepared for this, for a complication, there remained a piece of me desperate to believe it had all been a big mistake. I longed to cradle her precious softness into my skin and ached to breathe in her new baby smell as I felt her heartbeat against mine. I wanted to hear her soft, quick breath in my ear and experience visits from happy smiling friends in contrast to hugs of sympathy and comfort.

"So it wasn't a dream?" Sadness clung to my question.

"No, Sunshine. It wasn't a dream."

"Why, Mom? Why can't I, just once, have a healthy baby so many mothers get to experience?"

She sat on my bed and snuggled next to me. Short arms wrapped around me, trying to smooth away the hurt. "I'm so sorry, sweetheart. You're grieving for an experience you've lost. We can carry our wants and plans in our hearts, but when they don't coexist with God's, the result can be hard to accept. We don't always know why things happen the way they do or what the end result will mean for our lives, but we can aim to find peace and hope in the belief that God has a plan for our suffering. The purpose of our pain may not be revealed for years, but it is not in vain. The struggle is intentional."

I tucked my head into her neck and breathed in her familiar fragrance. Defeated and exhausted, I longed to hide forever in the protection of her love. Huddled in her arms, I could face anything. God had sent me an angel, and she was here next to me.

After a few moments, I finally lifted my head toward her. Her face, though always lightened with hope, seemed to illuminate. I could feel my body relax, beginning at my core before I spoke. "His plan, not mine. Right?"

"Right."

Her arms enveloped my shoulders with a final hug. "Now, we should go see your baby."

I looked down at my feet. "I'd love to, but I still can't move my legs." I chuckled—a foreign sensation given the gravity of my current situation. I welcomed the feeling.

"Sunshine," her giggle light and infectious, "even in the depth of such sadness, you manage to find laughter. I'm so proud of you. Your little family may have a tough road ahead, but always remember the beautiful gift you were granted. God's own admission, 'Everything is going to be okay.'"

She unwrapped her arms from my shoulders and shimmied from the bed.

"Where are you going?" I felt a twinge of panic where the previous warmth had been.

Sensing my fear, she rested her hand on my shoulder. "I'm just going to find your nurse. I'm sure they can take you in a wheelchair. You need to see Sophia." Nearly out the door, she turned back. Her face peeked beyond the metal frame. "She's beautiful, by the way."

Ghost-like, she disappeared out the door. On my lap lay my quilt with its mixed colors and bold patterns. I stroked the fabric beneath my fingers, exploring each stitch as it brushed my skin. Each new texture told a story of love from my mother to those she adored so much. Like the thread of the quilt, she was our matriarch, our cornerstone, holding us all together.

Moments later, she returned with a chair and a nurse scurrying behind her. "Um, excuse me, Ma'am. What's the wheelchair for?"

Her mouth pulled tight across her teeth, displaying her mischievousness. "I'm gonna take my daughter to see her baby. Do you want to help me?" She turned quickly to the young nurse, daring her to offer anything but a confirmation of help.

I watched, stunned by Mom's atypical behavior.

The young nurse placed her hand lightly on Mom's arm. "Yes, Ma'am. I would love to help. There are just a couple of things we need to do before getting her out of bed, and then we can wheel her right down."

She leaned toward Mom, and I overheard her whisper. "We're on the same team."

Standing up straight, she winked and snapped her fingers. "All righty then. Let's get to it."

They quickly completed the few tasks needed to free me from my bed. The nurse disconnected my IV from the tubing and pushed the pole to the side. With Mom's help, they swung my legs until I was upright in the bed, legs dangling over the side. In this position, I could actually move more than I thought. It felt good to be doing something. Within moments, I was seated comfortably in the wheelchair.

"You ready?" She kissed the top of my head, a slight sadness drawing upon her face. A poker face was not in her repertoire. Even with her best efforts, she was unable to camouflage the worry settled into the creases on her face.

I inhaled deeply, wanting to draw up every ounce of courage remaining in my weary body. I would need more than my own strength for what was coming next. "Heavenly Father. I need your strength. I sense the seriousness of the situation I'm about to face. Knowing it's your plan, please strengthen my battle-weary soul. Seal up my heart. Create a fortress of Your love, faith, and trust so I might go about this crusade ready for what may come. Help me find your peace, Lord. The peace that surpasses all understanding. And in the midst of the greatest battles, help me see your face. I will hold within my heart your words Lord—'everything is going to be okay,' and trust you fully understand their meaning.

Lord, watch over my sweet Sophia. I know she has hordes of angels surrounding her, ready to protect her at all times. Together, may we find your strength. In your Son Jesus' name. Amen."

Taking one final deep breath, I reached for my mother's hand. "I'm ready."

She gazed at me with all the love she held within her heart. "You are so strong, Sunshine, and I'm so proud of you. I will be with you always."

"I know, Mom." I tucked the quilt a little tighter over my lap. "You always are."

HIS PLAN, NOT MINE

I sensed her before I saw her, the severed cord of birth replaced by an invisible cord of love. Through the window of the nursery, I recognized the clear plastic oxygen tubing in her nose. Every cell in my body begged to run to her. I ached to place her tiny body next to mine and protect her from all the unknown.

As they opened the nursery door, the dissonance of babies crying and call lights ringing filled the four wooden walls. I vaguely heard the nurse's reminder to wait until I was closer before leaving the chair. "Just in case your legs aren't strong enough." In my stubbornness, I ignored them.

"I appreciate your concern, but they'll be fine. I just need to hold my baby." My body still ached from delivery. My legs, weakened from the epidural, threatened to defy me. But I reinforced my strength and willed myself out of the chair, stumbling slightly before I reached a seat next to her incubator.

"Momma's here, Sophia." My heart throbbed as I placed her warm body into my arms, never asking for permission. My need to hold her overtook any sense of courtesy toward the rules.

To an untrained observer, she looked well. But not to me. I recognized the bluish hue in her skin and the awkward way she gulped with each breath. She whimpered, tired of struggling to breathe outside the safety of my womb. Her cheeks were swollen, evidence of the fluid collecting inside her.

"Hi, sweet baby. I know you're hurting. Mommy and Daddy will do everything we can to get you healthy and keep you safe. We love you so much precious

Sophia." The suffering within me threatened to break my last fragment of composure. "The doctors will find out what's wrong and make you all better. Momma will *never* stop fighting for you."

I could sense my mom's gentle hand on my shoulder. I needed her strength as much as Sophia needed mine. Three generations of love cocooned in one thin line.

Lost in my own thoughts, I saw the doctor before I heard his words. My heart sank. His face was familiar from our previous stay in the NICU with Lillian. If he were involved, her condition would not be a simple fix. As he spoke, his thick accent blurred the words in my fragile mind. I knew he was trying to explain something of importance. In my fog, his statements arrived broken like a bad radio signal.

"Chest x-ray . . . big cystic structure . . ." I watched his lips move, begging my brain to catch up to his words. "Unsure of the cause…likely CPAM. We'll have the pediatric surgeon come and speak with you." I stared at him. Though his mouth was moving, his face remained blurry, as if obscured by fog.

Questions raced through my mind. *What is he talking about? Big cyst? Where? He said chest x-ray. It must be her lungs. Did he say CPAM? What in the world is CPAM? Why would we need a surgeon? Is that even what he said?*

Panic quickened my breath. My heart thumped hard against my sternum. The doctor continued to speak, but his words could not cut through the siren in my ears. *Lord, why does he keep talking. I don't even understand what he's saying. Please make him stop.*

My mother's hand, still on my shoulder, gave me a gentle squeeze shifting me back to reality. I gave my head a hard shake. *Pull it together, Sonya.* Instinctively, I pulled Sophia closer, protecting her from the gravity of his words.

I spoke, interrupting whatever thought he was finishing. "I'm sorry, Sir. I'm still feeling a little foggy." I pointed a weak, trembling finger toward my head. "I'm not sure I caught all the details. Did I hear you say she has a cyst on her lungs? And you mentioned something about a surgeon. Why would she need one of those?"

I willed myself to listen intently to each word, knowing Sophia's very life depended on them. He continued, his heavy accent making it even more difficult for me to focus. "Yes. On the chest x-ray, there is a large air-filled space occupying the majority of her chest. We can't tell from the x-ray exactly what the lesion is or how much of the lungs are affected, but it appears to be coming from her right lung. The size of the defect is causing a lot of deviation of other structures within her chest."

Other structures within her chest. Heart, lungs, trachea, esophagus—all vital for life. I nodded in understanding, though I had only absorbed bits of what he described. *Think Sonya. I know you're tired, but you have got to pull it together.* Before he could turn to walk away, I stopped him. "Sir. Did you say something about a surgeon?"

"Yes. When the cyst is exceptionally large, like your baby's, it often requires surgical removal. I have a consult set with the pediatric surgeon to discuss those details with you."

He looked down at Sophia then back to me. "Did you know about this abnormality before birth? Was it visible at your twenty-week ultrasound?"

I shook my head quickly. "No, the OB said everything was normal, and it was. I saw the images."

He shrugged. "Surprising. Usually, masses this big show up on the ultrasound."

Masses this big. I stared at him for a moment, willing him to change his story. In my heart, I knew he wasn't describing another infant. He wasn't explaining the scene of heartbreak another family would have to endure. He was talking about my baby, describing my heartbreak.

I pulled her closer to me, building an invisible barrier around her innocence. I wanted to protect her. But as much as I needed to shelter her from the trauma, I realized I couldn't take this from her. I could only be there through every difficult moment.

The steady beep of her oxygen sensor began to slow, a sound I recognized from my years working in the operating room. The decreased pace and tone meant her saturation had dropped. The gravity of the future left me numb. As my eyes lifted, I noticed a small crowd of nurses ready to transfer her to the NICU. I secured one last moment to hold my baby tight. Joe stepped next to me as we surrounded Sophia with our love.

Sensing my fragile state, Mom put her head next to mine. "I can feel your heart breaking, Sunshine, and mine breaks for you. Remember God's words spoken to you through the woman at church. 'Everything is going to be okay.' Remember those words. 'His plan, not yours.'"

Nodding slightly, I pressed quivering lips to my baby's face. I felt her newness, her soft, innocent skin. "My sweet Sophia. They're going to take you for a while, but I'll come as soon as they let me. We all love you so much. God is with you, little one. Be strong, my baby."

Lifting her toward the nurse, her warmth no longer filled my arms. I was empty, drained of all life. I lowered myself into the chair and searched for Joe.

He leaned into my neck. "Everything's going to be okay. Whatever that means, we have to trust that."

Defeated, I slunk myself into the cold, hard wheelchair. I sheltered my eyes as we rolled down the hall. Unwilling to witness the joyful faces of new parents gleefully pushing their newborns. When we reached my hospital room, it felt barren, devoid of the new life that belonged there. I recoiled against the emptiness. A rush of anger rose within me like flames of fire ready to spread. I demanded answers.

Finding my phone, I punched in my password. Pulling up a browser, I frantically typed "CPAM" into the search bar. My heart hammered in my angst to know more. I needed to understand what was happening.

Mom sat next to me in a side chair, her eyes downcast and tormented with silent tears. The pain in her features spoke volumes. "Sunshine, I know you are hurting and searching for answers right now. Please remember, sometimes the answers we need aren't found in a search bar. They're found with God. Even as I speak these warnings, I know you need to understand. You need the knowledge and answers the medical community knows. Be careful, Sunshine. Tread lightly. The explanations you receive from the outside can be the source of further pain, in contrast to the hope-filled responses of God."

She smiled weakly and closed her eyes, waiting, knowing her advice couldn't stop me.

After what seemed an eternity, results populated my screen. I scanned them quickly, choosing a reputable site. Hungry for information, I flipped through the words. Each message was the same. "Congenital Pulmonary Airway Malformation . . . rare disease . . . a mass of abnormal fetal lung tissue . . . no known case . . . severity varies greatly . . . severe cases often fatal."

The final word fragmented my heart like a stray bullet. Instant searing pain radiated throughout my body. My postpartum imbalance left me delirious, unable to comprehend the words scrolling through my head fully. One line repeatedly flashed like a neon sign on its last minutes of life. "Severe cases often fatal."

I threw my phone across the bed. Flinging my head back on the pillow, I wept, trying to empty myself of all the pain. I released my hurt and anger in immense, ugly sobs. Still sitting next to me, Joe wrapped his arm around me. I buried my head into him. "It says large masses could be fatal. God said everything was going to be okay. Fatal is not okay. Fatal means I don't get to take my baby home. Fatal doesn't work for me."

Mom rose from her chair. Reaching me, she combed her fingers through my hair. "We have to keep the faith, Sunshine. Remember His plan, not ours."

I snapped my head toward her, snarling. "I don't want *His* plan, Mom. I want my plan. I want to hold my innocent little baby in my arms and kiss her and smile at her noises. Don't you see? I don't want *His* plan."

She stroked my cheek. Like heat thawing ice, her touch began to melt the anger and hardness I'd erected. She cupped my face. "I know you don't want His plan now. You may not even see its worth in a few months or a couple of years. But I promise, you will see a purpose for all your pain. For now, just rest. Close your eyes and rest."

I was drained. My womb was empty, and so was my soul. I didn't know how much more I could handle. Taking her advice, I closed my eyes. Before drifting into sleep's reprieve, I offered a silent plea.

"Dear Lord. I'm frightened and devastated. Please hold me and give me strength. Breathe faith in my lungs and release my fear. Please be with me."

A PEACE WORTH FIGHTING FOR

The phone blared from the corner as I woke disoriented. In moments, I realized where I was. The emptiness hollowed me. "Sophia." Searching for the phone, I finally picked up after the third ring.

"Hello?" My voice cracked with the edge of sleep.

"Mrs. Mack? This is Dr. Sinclair from the NICU. I'm taking care of your daughter, Sophia, today."

My body ached at the sound of her name, further carving into the emptiness.

"Sophia was having some difficulty breathing, and her blood gases indicated her oxygen level was low. We had to place her on a ventilator, and her vital signs are stable now."

I gripped the phone. *A ventilator.* I took a moment to compose myself before responding. "Is she stable otherwise? Do you have any more information about her prognosis?"

She paused before answering. Even her brief moment of silence was enough for me to understand the gravity of Sophia's situation. "I'm sorry, Mrs. Mack, we'll have to take it one day at a time. The cyst is rather large, and it appears to have caused the remaining lobes of her lungs to collapse. It's just too early to know if her remaining lung tissue is normal or not."

My head spun—like too many rides on the carousel. I hated the twirling sensation and the nauseous, disoriented feeling that accompanied it. I grasped the bed railing and willed the spinning to stop.

"Mrs. Mack? Are you still there?"

"Yes, Doctor. I'm sorry." I steadied myself trying to extract the dizziness. *You can do this, Sonya. Think medical. You can break down later, not now.*

Mom must have noticed my internal torment because she stood from her small bed and sat near me. "I'm right here."

Consoled by her presence, I turned my attention back to the phone. "You said her lungs may not be normal. Are you saying her lungs may never reinflate?" A thousand questions scrolled through my head.

"There is the potential. There are a lot of unknowns right now. We administered steroids which appear to have helped her saturations. We think the cyst may be contained to only one lobe of her lungs, but the capacity of the remaining lung tissue is still unclear. It will take us a few days to work out if the cyst will decrease on its own or if she will require surgery to remove the diseased portion of her lung."

My head swirled again and another wave of nausea struck me. I understood her medical jargon and the information she conveyed was bad. With five lobes between both sides of her lungs, it wasn't yet clear if removing the cystic structure would allow the rest of her lungs to expand and take over. What would it mean if her lungs didn't reinflate? Would she have to be on a ventilator her whole life? Would she need a lung transplant? Would she survive?

I struggled not to slip down the slope of what-ifs and whys. How would I survive if my baby didn't? I'd already endured the unfathomable loss of someone I loved so intensely. Would I really have to suffer so exquisitely again?

All the emotions swirled in my head like a tornado, threatening the total destruction of all in its path.

"Mrs. Mack? Did I lose you again?" The doctor's voice was patient.

"I'm sorry. It's a lot to take in. When can I see her?" I longed to touch her and let her know I was near. I wanted to tell her everything was going to be all right. Even if there was a chance that it wasn't.

"I know the surgeon is on his way to see you. Why don't you wait until you talk to him and then make your way up here."

"Is it Dr. Devi?"

"Yes."

I'd known Dr. Devi professionally for years. Hearing his name was a small comfort in the midst of tremendous heartache. "Okay. I'll wait until I see him. Thank you."

There was a brief pause before she began to say goodbye. "Dr. Sinclair? One more thing if I could."

"Yes."

I knew the protocol of most providers. Sometimes, especially in the light of the unknown, there may be details left unsaid to the families so as not to worry them unnecessarily until, as the provider, you had more of the answers. "Is there anything you aren't telling me? Anything you wouldn't normally tell the parents yet, but you might tell a colleague or consulting physician?"

"No, Mrs. Mack. I assure you. If we knew more, I would tell you. Dr. Devi will decide if she needs a CT scan to understand further the gravity of the situation. But for now, you know what I know."

"Thank you for your honesty, Dr. Sinclair. And Doctor?"

"Yes," even in her one word, I could hear her sympathy.

"Please take care of my little girl."

"We'll do everything we can to keep her safe."

The signal beeped, ending the call. My head sunk as tears streamed endlessly down my face. Joe shifted himself to be next to me. Snuggling into me, I knew he wanted to know what she'd said, but I was in no shape to rehash it.

From my other side, Mom's tears reflected mine. I couldn't bear all the pain in the room. There was a pain so heavy I feared the walls might shatter from its weight.

After a few moments of silence, I braced to speak. My words sounded foreign. They broke from the voice of someone tormented by anguish, not the joyful banter of a new mother. "They said she's on the ventilator and aren't sure how much of her lung tissue is healthy." Each sentence was a burden I felt unable to bear. "It might only be in one lobe, but there are too many unknowns right now." I paused, summoning more courage. "I asked if I could see her, but they want me to wait for the surgeon to arrive because he's on his way."

I could feel my composure crack like a dam holding back the massive waters of a river, too long neglected. At first, it was steady, but each word added pressure to an unstable barrier.

"Are you okay?" At Mom's question, the flood whooshed forward. I collapsed into a heap of brokenness on the bed. Her voice reminded me of everything I was missing up in that tiny hospital room. The bond between a mother and a daughter is so strong that nothing could break it. Unsure what to do, my family watched silently as my facade crumbled. It shattered into a million shards upon the floor as the floodwaters of my sorrow broke forward.

I let them rush. I wanted the gush of tears to wash away the sadness that engulfed me and longed for the peace to fill the space within me that remained in the brokenness. I didn't care how I seemed on the outside or what level of composure I appeared to maintain. The pain had overtaken me, and I didn't care who witnessed it.

I felt my mother's presence next to me while my body heaved. Too long had I carried the burden of the unknown, and even now, in the light of the known, the pressure was too much to bear.

"I don't understand." My voice wailed, ringing off the surface of the pale yellow walls. "Why? Why can't I finally have a healthy baby? Why does my baby have to be up there struggling to survive?" I pointed a sharp finger toward the ceiling, indicating the location of the NICU where Sophia lay fighting for her life.

I snapped my head toward Mom, giving her a sharp stare. "*You* know God so well. Why is He doing this?"

It wasn't her fault. I knew that. No one was to blame. But I wanted, *needed*, someone to condemn for how I was feeling.

"Sunshine." Even her voice, like ointment soothing the wounds of a hurt child, couldn't camouflage the misery on her face. Throughout my entire life, she'd graciously offered to relieve every burden that lay on my shoulders. This was no different. She knew she could never physically remove the pain I felt, and that was anguish enough for her. "Sonya. You know I would take your heartbreak if I could. Your hurt and worry are so deep, and those emotions are understandable. But in times of trial, we can't focus on the why. 'Why' is a question you may never know this side of heaven. What you must concentrate on instead are the promises God has already provided." She shifted her body to face me; sympathy contorted her features.

"He promises a reward for our faith and trust—a peace that surpasses all understanding. And most importantly, He promises you a love beyond any you can imagine. His heart is hurting for you, just as your heart is breaking for Sophia. Never lose sight of that. His love for you is overwhelming and never-ending. It is beyond anything you could ever imagine." She smoothed a strand of hair, tucking it behind my ear, then wiped a stray tear from my cheek.

"Ever since you were little, you've climbed up onto my lap. Even when you were too big, and it seemed unrealistic." She chuckled reverently at the memory. "You always claimed it made you feel safe somehow like the world couldn't get to you. Right now, you need to climb up onto God's lap. Nuzzle your head into His shoulder and feel His loving arms around you. There's no pain or heartbreak that He can't ease when you trust Him. The journey might be rocky and downright scary, but in His arms, you can rest and know you're safe."

Each word soothed the brokenness scattered across the floor. I wasn't sure how much time had passed before my breathing began to slow. The pressure of sadness was muted but still present. I lifted my body wearily from the bed.

Crawling across the hospital sheets, I maneuvered myself onto her lap. As it always had, the world seemed to fall away when I was near her. Her vanilla fragrance and gentle breath soothed my aching pieces.

"I know you're right, Mom. None of this is His fault, or my fault, or anyone's for that matter. It's just easier to blame someone else when my life has shattered into a million pieces.

"But the good news is," I reached a hand toward Joe, grateful for the two pillars of strength sitting next to me. "I have you two to help me through. It's like you said, 'the reward for our faith and trust is a peace that surpasses all understanding.'"

DISCONNECT

So this is it. The starched, white sheets of my hospital bed were tucked up around my chin, and I willed them to provide protection against the upcoming emotional battle. "Others have been here, navigating unfamiliar terrain of a sick baby, with the weight of burden on their boots. Don't focus so much on the difficult path or unknown ground, Sonya. Keep your eyes on your Guide." My plea whispered into the room.

I stared blankly out the window at the traffic on the streets. Hundreds of people traveled their familiar routes to places they had been to countless times before. I envied their predictiveness.

Lost in the silence of my thoughts, I hardly heard the gentle knock at the door. Dr. Devi's quiet Indian accent floated into the room. "Hello? Can I come in?"

I glanced at a mirror on the wall. My face wrinkled in disapproval. Red hair jutted aimlessly from a messy ponytail on the top of my head. My eyes, swollen and crimson from crying, appeared unrecognizable. "I look like I've been through a war." I shrugged. "In a way, I have."

Raising my voice, I called to the door. "Yeah, we're here. Come in."

I sat up quickly, trying to summon the remaining composure locked somewhere in the depths of my body.

He shook my hand as he passed by in his green scrubs. I looked at the clock. 5:30 in the evening. "Long day in the OR." I thought before he shuffled toward a chair tucked into the corner of the room. He pulled it closer, settling in.

His gesture was not lost. All my years in the hospital have taught me most doctors don't relax in the presence of patients. Sitting was personal and intimate, not the rapid-paced demeanor they usually projected. But he wasn't just another unknown doctor. He was a friend.

"How're you holding up?" He spoke softly, as if anything louder might fracture my remaining strength.

"I've had better days, but I'm doing okay right now. I wasn't expecting to see a surgeon after delivering my baby." Forcing back tears, I inhaled sharply. "But I'm grateful it's you and not some stranger."

He nodded his head silently, waiting for me to continue.

"Have you had a chance to see her?" I asked.

"Yes, I stopped up there first. They're getting ready to do an echo."

My own heart stopped for a beat. Dr. Sinclair hadn't mentioned anything about an echocardiogram, an ultrasound of her heart. "Is there something wrong with her heart? I thought the only problem was her lungs." My voice raised an octave, sounding unfamiliar.

He shook his head gently. Each movement was meant to declare calmness. "No. It's more of a precaution. The cyst is taking up a lot of space, and they want to check all the surrounding structures."

I felt the familiar sting in my eyes, a precursor to tears that threatened to betray me. Sensing the breach, Mom snuggled up next to me in the bed, a shield against the potential onslaught of bad news.

"Dr. Devi?" Despite my best effort, my voice quaked with the weight of the question that threatened to suffocate me. I was afraid to ask for fear that merely speaking the word might bring it to fruition. I looked into his dark eyes, simultaneously wanting the truth and a lie that would ease my heartbreak. "Is she going to die?"

There it was again—the familiar cracking of my fortitude. Stray tears defied me. Ignoring them, I kept my focus on him.

"Sonya, why ask such a question? I know it seems bad right now, but we must take this one step at a time."

The words rushed out like a river breaking free from the dam. I couldn't stop them, let alone filter them. My thoughts came continuously, one extended question.

"Well, that doctor in the nursery, he said something about CPAM, and I don't even know what CPAM is. So I Googled it, and I tried to read only the medically responsible pages, but even those scared me. They said most of the time, it resolved or didn't cause issues, but in children with large cysts, it could be fatal. Then that doctor upstairs said it was really large, and they didn't know if her other lung tissue was healthy. She is already on a ventilator, and you and I both know that's not a good sign. I'm sitting here and don't know anything. I don't like being on this side of things. So I am asking you, is she going to die?" My shoulders, weary from all the hurt and fear resting there, hung defeated.

He waited a moment, the silence hanging between us. I braced myself for his response. "I don't know how many times I have to tell them they need to disconnect the Wi-Fi from the labor and delivery floor. Postpartum women should not be allowed to Google."

I stared at him, stunned. And then it hit me. Laughter. Light and free, like the weight of a thousand years lifted off my shoulders. It drifted forward, filling the room. I wasn't sure if I was laughing because it was funny or because I was delirious, but it felt good to breathe again. For the first time in months, I felt a brief moment of freedom.

"Man, I am a hot mess," I mumbled, making sure no one could hear, then collected myself before addressing him again. "Did you seriously just say that?" I couldn't help but smile, feeling how easily my breath came.

"Well, it's true. Women should not be looking up serious material moments after delivering a baby. It's too much. But, I will tell you what I know. I have taken a look at the chest x-ray, and the cyst does look rather large. It is causing some pressure on other structures, but we don't know its significance yet. We will likely need to order a CT scan, but I would like to give her the night to stabilize before we try and transport her down there for the test. It will also give us time to see if the cystic lung tissue will shrink because that happens occasionally."

He gently crunched himself forward, elbows on his knees, hands folded in his lap. "If we have to do the CT scan tomorrow, we will. If we have to do surgery to take it out, we will. If surgery is required, I will make sure Dr. Holloway is around to join me."

Dr. Holloway was a well-known and respected pediatric heart surgeon, and we were lucky to have him in our Midwestern city. Even if an operation were required, I knew Sophia would be in the capable hands of two highly skilled surgeons.

Relaxing further into his chair, Dr. Devi folded his hands and placed them on his lap. His calm demeanor relaxed me. "So what I am telling you is, we will know more tomorrow. But for today, go upstairs and see your baby. See how she is resting comfortably, even if it's with the aid of the ventilator. She is in the best place she can be. And if the time comes for us to operate, we will do everything we can to keep her safe."

My heart knew he was right. This was the plan all along. God's plan. Take it one day at a time. Trust. Faith. Peace.

"Thank you, Dr. Devi. I sincerely appreciate you coming by when you have already had a long day."

He waved a hand toward me, "No problem."

He shook my hand once more, then, starting to leave, stopped just shy of the door. Pulling a paper towel off the holder on the wall, he snatched a pen from his pocket and scribbled something on the paper. "If you need anything tonight, or think of any questions, call me." He handed me the paper towel. "This is my cell phone number. Don't be afraid to use it."

"Thank you."

"You're welcome. I'll see you tomorrow. Okay?"

"Okay." As he turned to leave the room, I looked from Joe to Mom. I knew they had a lot of questions. When talking to doctors, I always took for granted that I could fill in the blanks that often confused those without medical backgrounds. But I was spent. There was no endurance left in me for more questions or worry.

Without saying a word to either of them, I searched the bed for my call light. Finding the box, I pushed the red button with the nurse symbol. Within seconds, a voice came through the box. "Can I help you?"

"Yes. I want to go see my baby."

BRACE FOR IMPACT

've never been on a plane about to crash, tons of steel barreling toward the ground as cries for help echo over the engine's roar. Just before the plane hits, the pilot calls out one final warning, "Ladies and gentleman, brace for impact."

As I stood just outside the partially closed hospital door, my newborn fighting for her life on the other side, I sensed I knew what it felt like to have your life hurtling toward the ground with nothing to stop it.

Stepping closer to the door, I froze instantly, hearing voices on the other side.

"How's the echo looking?" The question originated from an unfamiliar voice.

"A small amount of pulmonary hypertension. But that's normal in a newborn. Otherwise, her heart looks good."

"Dr. Lang," I whispered. This voice I knew. Dr. Lang was a pediatric heart doctor I had gotten to know over the years. His genuine quietude and calm demeanor made him an easy favorite for many of his patients. "Another good one, Lord. Thank you."

Having good doctors was monumental in a case like Sophia's. Not just physicians with skill and intelligence, but an equally important bedside manner.

Taking one last breath to steady myself before entering, I nearly crashed into Dr. Lang as he exited.

"Oh." He put his hand on his heart, startled. "Hey." His smile remained warm and compassionate despite the late hour.

"Hello, Dr. Lang. Didn't mean to scare you."

"No problem. I should have been watching where I was going." Truly seeing me, his previously jovial expression morphed to one of sympathy. The gesture, though kind, served to remind me of the situation. "Rough day, huh?" He tapped me gently on the shoulder.

"I guess it shows, huh?" I hadn't glanced in the mirror lately, but given that my body felt I'd endured a plane crash, I was sure my face reflected all signs of the exhaustion I felt. I could feel the swollenness around my eyes. My hair was a mess, and my shoulders were permanently slumped forward, like a ragdoll who'd taken too many turns in the dryer.

I lowered my head, releasing our eye contact. Exhaling loudly, I tried to let out the pressure that was building again. "Do you have some good news for me? I could really use some."

Glancing quickly at his face, I caught the edge of a smile. *That's promising. Usually, they don't smile if they're going to tell you bad news.*

"Yes, actually. Her heart looks strong. Just a little pulmonary hypertension, but that's normal in newborns. If her lungs were all non-functioning or underdeveloped, I would expect the pressures to be much higher."

I lifted my eyes and forced myself to smile. "That is really good news." And though it was, there remained too much unknown to celebrate.

He continued, eager to deliver more positive results. "Sounds like they'll probably do a scan tomorrow to get a better picture of her lungs. But for now, they have her lying on her left side to see if taking the pressure off that lung will help it reinflate.

Hearing a sniffle behind me, I glanced back. I had almost forgotten Joe and Mom were standing there with confused looks on their faces, lost in medical jargon. "I'll explain later," I mouthed before turning my attention back to the doctor.

I reached a hand out toward him, which he quickly grasped. "I sincerely appreciate you coming so late."

"No problem. I'm sorry you have to go through this." He gestured toward Sophia's room.

"Me too. But I'm relieved to have such incredible doctors."

Still shaking my hand, he placed his other hand on my shoulder. "That's very kind of you. Please don't hesitate to let me know if you have any questions." He gave my shoulder one final pat before he turned to walk away down the hallway.

Taking a moment to collect myself, I closed my eyes. My head pounded from the tears I'd shed throughout the day. It was as if my body could fall asleep at any moment.

I turned slowly toward my companions. Mom spoke first. "Can you explain?"

I chuckled lightly. I was surprised how even the smallest laugh could ease the built-up anxiety.

"Yes. Pulmonary hypertension is high blood pressure caused by a problem with the lungs rather than the body, like if they aren't functioning well for some reason. It can be normal in new babies. Newborns haven't had to use their lungs in the womb because they received oxygen from the umbilical cord. In essence, he's saying if more than just the one area of her lungs were bad, the high pressures would be much worse. Thankfully, he said that her heart looked good."

Relief replaced the confusion on their faces. "Oh, that's good news." Mom clasped her hands together, giving a loud sigh of relief.

"Definitely is." I smiled briefly. "Sounds like we'll know more tomorrow after the CT scan."

I glanced toward Joe. The usual sparkle in his eyes appeared muted as if the last few hours had forever changed them. Regret washed over me. I felt selfish. Lost in my own agony of the recent events, I'd neglected to fully comprehend how they might have affected him. I knew these doctors, worked with them regularly, and understood their words. But all of this was unfamiliar, frightening terrain for him.

I sensed the same fear that encapsulated me. On instinct, I touched him. "You doing okay?"

Since the moment we'd met, he existed as my protector. He was always aware of my emotions, even when they shifted as readily as the sand on the shoreline. I knew he wouldn't break down, not here, not as I had. But as a single tear traced his cheek, I understood the instability of his resolve.

He gently squeezed my hand, giving me a half-hearted smile. "I'm good." Though his eyes betrayed his words, I knew this was not the moment to press him further.

Keeping my firm grip on his hand, we turned to face the door. I had knocked on these hospital doors countless times, but standing here now, I saw its humble exterior from a new perspective. No longer was I the provider coming to heal, but rather the patient praying for healing.

I felt Mom's presence beside me, a guardian angel of protection safeguarding my heart. Familiar sounds of the monitored vital signs drifted toward me. The unbroken beep of the oxygen monitor. The quiet pump and release as the machine monitored her blood pressure. One sound resonated above them all. Its persistent rhythm drew up previously sealed wounds—the mechanical breath of the ventilator. "*Whish, whoosh, hum. Whish, whoosh, hum.*"

I steadied myself, grasping the door. Drawing in a deep, steady breath, I summed up all my strength and pressed my eyes closed in silent prayer.

I need you, Lord. I know what's coming in the next few days will test my courage, my strength, and, most importantly, my faith. Stay with me. I beg you. Make evident Your presence and promise to guide me through every battle in this war. Faith. Trust. Peace. Grant me your peace when my heart wants to fail. Help me to see your hand, God. Let me always remember this is Your plan—not mine. Stay with me, God. Please.

I placed a hand on the large wooden door, then turning to face Joe, I whispered. "Let's go see our baby."

THE VERSE

There are moments that will alter your life forever. Visions you can't unsee and words you can't unhear become forever imprinted in your memory. As I lay in my hospital room the night Sophia was born, staring into the blackness, the image beyond the closed NICU door burned into my mind. My innocent baby lay motionless, except for the predictable cadence of the ventilator expanding her lungs. Cords and wires covered nearly every surface of her body, connecting her to monitors that displayed her vital signs. A tiny tube, smaller than a drinking straw, extruded from her mouth. In stark contrast to the sterile medical devices, a miniature pink hat with a bow trimmed her head.

Nothing could have stopped me from going to her. I was magnetized by an invisible force to be near her. My vision tunneled at the edges, focused only on my baby. Stepping next to her bed, I reached my hand to feel her face. Her cheeks were warm and silky beneath my fingers. I longed to pick her up, to feel her next to me.

I stood next to her for nearly an hour before the nurses politely suggested I get some sleep. In exhaustion, I took their advice. But even in the comfort of an actual bed, my mind was full of swirling thoughts, but my body felt empty. Joe occupied the space next to me. I was jealous of his sleep and the reprieve it granted him.

Tomorrow would be a big day. Sophia was scheduled for her scan, and we would have more answers and better direction. Longing to empty my mind, to find reprieve in the sweet embrace of sleep, I closed my eyes, willing myself to sleep.

The night was restless. I woke many times, panicked, feeling as if I had lost something important. I hoisted myself up in the bed. Glancing around, I saw only the same austere walls of my empty hospital room. Pressing my head back to the pillow, I imagined Sophia laying two floors above me. I yearned to go to her but knew the doctors and nurses were taking good care of her. Sleep was what I needed now. I knew from my previous stay in the NICU with Lillian that sleeping was a near impossibility. Nurses and doctors constantly entered the room, checked vital signs, and attended to rounds while noises echoed, alarms rang, and lights shone in corners of the room.

I needed something to distract my mind, so I began to pray. Somewhere among the silent repetitive nature of verses I'd known since childhood, I drifted into sleep.

My phone alarm chirped at seven a.m., the time of Sophia's scan. I knew the doctors would round soon after, and I was determined to be present when they arrived.

After a quick brush of my hair, I tossed it into a messy bun on the crown of my head. Glancing hastily into the mirror, I grimaced at my appearance. My eyes, bloodshot and swollen, were only a trace of what they'd once been. Combined with my cheeks, still puffy from the fluid given during delivery and the extra weight I gained during pregnancy, I didn't recognize myself.

I splashed some water on my face and patted it dry before applying the smallest amount of makeup. I stared into the mirror as I brushed my teeth. *One of these days, you're going to need to shower, Sonya.*

Throwing on some clothes I found in my suitcase, I gave Joe a quick kiss on the way out the door, waking him up. "Hey, aren't you going to wait for me?" He called as I neared the exit.

"I'll meet you up there. I just want to make sure I'm there if the doctor rounds early. Her test was scheduled for seven, so I'm sure she's still in the scanner." I rushed out the door before he could object. In truth, I was desperate for some time alone to collect my thoughts before the doctor arrived.

Still feeling the sting of delivery, I opted for the elevator. As the door opened, the familiar mechanical voice chimed. "Second floor. Going up." I stepped into the small space and stared ahead as the doors closed behind me. One step closer to seeing my baby again.

"Fourth floor. Going down." As the doors opened, I exited into the NICU waiting room. Small chairs and tables overlooked one of the best views of the city I called home. The sprawling landscape had transformed into a vibrantly growing municipality of trendy shops and restaurants over the years. Miles of buildings, homes, and roadways stretched out before me. The sun's rays glinted off the gold dome of the capitol building. Traffic moved freely as heat radiated off the black pavement. I spotted a Bible on a table and ran my hand over the rough cover, noticing the wear on its edges. Flipping through the pages, I saw various colors of ink underlying individual verses.

"This has to belong to someone." I thought briefly about putting it down, afraid the owner would return while I read. There was an intimacy in those pages I feared I might violate. But I couldn't bring myself to release it. It was as if the book had called to me. As I scanned the pages, one verse, in particular, would not be ignored.

"I'll read one verse, but then I'm putting it back."

The once black letters were now a soft gray with time and use. The pen marks beneath each line were smudged, the ink long rubbed away by fingers as they traced each line. I read each word slowly, digesting them individually.

"Proverbs 3:5–6. 'Trust in the Lord with all your heart, and lean not on your own understanding. In all your ways submit to Him, and He will make your paths straight.'"

I ran my finger over the verse as if touching the words would infuse them into the part of my soul that needed them. My mom's voice resounded in my ear, *Jesus is such a gentleman.*

"You're right, Mom. He's a true gentleman." Holding the book close to my heart, I closed my eyes, breathing in the words. Since the beginning of my pregnancy, I'd felt His presence. Amid pain or fear, I often lost sight of His words, but He was always there, graciously reinvesting His love in my heart.

Gently, I closed the book and situated it back down on the table. "I know you're here, Lord. Today's going to be a big day. Please stay with me. Show me this is Your plan. Grant me faith, trust, and peace."

I gazed once again out the vast glass window. A tiny yellow butterfly fluttered nearby, vying for my attention. I watched it carefully, mesmerized by its movements. Minutes passed, as I admired the majestic nature of her wings. My attention broke as the elevator chimed. "Fourth floor. Going down."

The doors parted as the sun, cresting above the golden dome, shone brightly through the window. Into the glare of the sun's rays, Mom stepped off the elevator.

"Good Morning, Sunshine. Are you ready for the big day?"

THE RESULTS

"**D**o you want to hold her?" The question came from Sophia's nurse. A middle-aged woman, probably around fifty with short blond hair and sympathetic eyes, stood over Sophia as I entered. A veteran, she moved swiftly around the room, without evidence of the trepidation I'd witnessed in a few of the less experienced nurses.

My heart leaped. I'd been longing to hold my baby since the moment they took her from my arms nearly a day ago.

"Can I?" I blurted it out quickly, afraid she would change her mind if I didn't answer soon enough.

"You sure can. Get situated over there in that chair, and I'll make sure all the cords and wires can reach. Make sure you're comfortable, because once you're holding her, she's going to stay there for a while. As long as she's doing well, of course." Her tone was serious but kind.

"Thank you so much." I smiled, hoping the expression would reflect my appreciation.

"You're welcome, honey. Babies belong with their mommas. They like it better than that crib anyway. You'll see." Her knowledge declared her experience.

Not wanting to miss my chance, I settled myself into the oversized chair in the corner. It wasn't very comfortable, too big for my torso. The cold vinyl shocked my skin. In all honesty, I knew it didn't matter what the seat was like. I just needed to hold my baby.

The nurse moved swiftly, unhooking the ventilator for the shortest amount of time as she situated Sophia's nearly naked body next to me. The moment her skin hit mine, the heat from her tiny body electrified my instincts.

"She likes it there. You see that?" The nurse pointed to the monitors. "Her heart and respiratory rates have already gone down to a more normal number than when she was laying in that crib. Like I said, babies are meant to be with their mommas."

I held her close, her head snuggled into the crook of my neck. I'd felt so empty, so barren in the previous hours, but feeling her soft skin and hearing her beating heart filled a blank space within me. Even covered in all the tubes, tape, and wires, she was still my living, breathing, beautiful gift from God. Holding her, I felt the chasm in my heart begin to heal.

Mom sat silently in the corner, her eyes filling with tears. "She's so beautiful. Perfectly and wonderfully made."

I smiled, understanding the reference to the famous Psalm. "Knitted together perfectly." I placed a kiss gently on Sophia's forehead, inhaling her sweetness. "God's got a special plan for you, Sophia. You and me. We just have to trust Him through it all. But no matter what, I'm going to be right here with you, baby girl. I will walk to the ends of the earth for you. Do you hear me, Sophia? I love you, baby. You and your sister are my little rays of sunshine."

Hearing the nickname she'd blessed me with since birth, Mom smiled. A single tear fell to the floor. We stared at each other silently, understanding the unwritten and often unspoken bond of motherhood. There was a sacredness that surpassed anything words could ever explain.

As I nestled further into the joy of holding my baby, the door opened. Joe appeared, freshly showered, but with evidence of worry on his face. "Did I miss the doctor?"

I shook my head, then snuggled it back down to Sophia's.

"They're letting you hold her." His declaration was a blend of happiness and envy. A recognizable example of what fatherhood should be, I understood the disappointment on his face.

I gave him a sympathetic look. "I'm sure they'll let you hold her, too. But I'm not giving her up yet, sorry." My face cracked a smile. It felt good, somehow lighter and freeing, to slowly become a closer version of the witty, happy person I used to be.

He situated himself next to me on a small hospital couch. Moving as near as he could, he reached his large hand and placed it on Sophia's bare skin. Her muscles flexed ever so slightly despite the haze of medication that sedated her.

Feeling her twitch, Joe's hand jerked back as if he'd placed it on a hot stove. "I'm sorry. Daddy didn't mean to scare you."

It amazed me how even his smallest gestures could awaken a renewed sense of love within me. I grabbed his hand, replacing it gently on Sophia's back. "I think your hand was just cold. Give it a second. Believe me; she wants to feel you're here just as much as you want to show her."

We remained that way, both of us relishing time with Sophia. The future sat like a stranger in the distance, unknown, unrecognized. None of us knew what was coming or the outcome, but we knew we were powerless to bring about what we wanted.

*****

Our solace was interrupted by a gentle knock at the door, Dr. Devi's voice rang in. "Can I come in?"

"Of course," nervousness betrayed the strength I'd hoped to convey. I was terrified to hear how the results of the CT scan would define our future.

He walked slowly into the room, glancing around for a chair but not finding one. He leaned awkwardly against the counter.

Breaking the silence, I blurted my question, "What did you find out?"

He studied me for a moment as if contemplating my emotional stability. "Well. The CT scan had some good news."

There was something about his tone, the quietness of it that relayed the unspoken. The good news would assuredly be followed by less favorable results. I remained silent, waiting for him to continue.

"The cyst is contained to one lobe of her lung, the right lower lobe, as we had suspected. Though it is large, the remainder of her lung tissue appears to be healthy, just some degree of atelectasis."

Joe looked at me, confused. "Atelectasis?"

I whispered into his ear. "It means deflated or collapsed. Her lung tissue is normal, just not expanded."

"But?" I implored him to tell the entire truth.

He looked down at Sophia, resting comfortably in my arms. A hint of sadness flashed across his face. I pulled her closer, trying to protect her from the gravity of his words.

He looked back up at me. "The cyst is large. So large, it's taking up too much room in her small chest. Her trachea, esophagus, and heart, all the vital structures in her thorax, are deviated because of its size. There is no room for her lungs to expand with the cyst there." He cleared his throat, preparing for the rest. "Usually, we try to leave these lesions in, let them spontaneously shrink, and then remove them if they're causing trouble down the road. We like to wait until a child is two or three, if we can. But Sophia can't wait that long. We have to remove it soon, so her remaining lung tissue has a chance to expand. Only after it is removed can we more fully assess how well her lungs are going to function."

I knew he was right. I knew if the cyst was truly as large as he was saying, it would need to come out.

"When?" I asked shyly, partly relieved there was something we could do besides sit and wait. The other part understood the extreme risks of operating on a baby so small and unstable. Experience had taught me that the difference between life and death could be a matter of millimeters in these infants.

"Tomorrow, probably." He paused, waiting for me to react. "I want to talk to Dr. Holloway and make sure that time will work for him. I'm comfortable doing the procedure, but it would be nice to have him around, just in case."

In case something goes wrong. I fought back the panic that threatened to expose my poised facade. He didn't need to finish his sentence. Dr. Holloway was a respected pediatric heart surgeon who was used to operating in the chest of tiny babies. If something went awry, he would be able to put her on ECMO, a machine that could keep her alive while her heart and lungs rested. Having them both present would help ease my fear. The question remained—*Would it be enough?*

I closed my eyes, rested my cheek on Sophia's face, and listened as the quiet whish of air filled her lungs and then retreated, pulsed by the ventilator. I couldn't raise my eyes or bring myself to look at Dr. Devi again. I knew there was always added pressure when you were operating on someone you knew, or even worse, their newborn.

"When will you know if we can do it tomorrow?"

His voice softened, making his Indian accent even more difficult to understand. I willed myself to listen closely. "Dr. Holloway is operating right now. I am waiting for him to finish." He turned to look at the clock, "It should be within the hour. When he is done, I will find out if he can join me tomorrow. If he can, that would be best. We are both going to be gone for the weekend due to the holiday."

Fourth of July. It hadn't even crossed my mind that in a few short days, millions would be celebrating the freedom of our country with fireworks and barbeques. At the same time, I found myself immersed in the battle to save my child's life.

I willed myself to look at him. "Thank you, doctor. I appreciate all your time and will wait for you to let me know."

He nodded his head, understanding nothing he could say would ease my heartbreak. Reaching out his hand, he placed it on Sophia's head. "We'll do everything we can to get her better."

Feeling the familiar sting in my eyes, I rushed to blink it away. "I know you will."

I watched as he disappeared behind the door. Sophia's hope for a normal future rested in the hands of two surgeons I'd admired and respected for years. I stared into the distance, the tiny room blurring around me.

Mom's voice broke my thoughts. "Are you okay, Sunshine?"

Shrugging my shoulders, I turned toward her. The tears I'd worked so hard to contain during Dr. Devi's visit broke forth.

"No." I cried, each tear releasing fear. "I'm scared. I know they're two of the best surgeons around, and this is what she needs," I gazed down at her pink face, "but I'm just so scared."

Finally, sitting in the safety of Joe and Mom, I allowed my hurt to release. "I feel so helpless. I hate being on the patient side of medicine. I'm used to being on that side." I pointed a sharp finger toward the door Dr. Devi had just exited.

"Oh, Sunshine." She stood from her end of the couch, crossing over to where I sat. Reaching me, she wrapped her arm around mine. The cocoon of safety began to wrap its way up my arm, encircling my entire body.

"Sonya, you know I'm not always good at saying exactly what I am trying to get across, but I'm going to try. Sometimes life can be really hard. It's a given. But God loves us so much. He wants to take our burdens if we let Him. You know I can't rattle off verses, but I know they're in the Bible. We've read them. His love and longing to bear our pain is something I feel so deeply it's etched on my heart. I've been through some pretty tough situations, but it was always His strength that got me through. Not mine."

She ran her fingers through the tuft of Sophia's blonde hair, then raising her eyes to mine, I noticed the way the light glinted off her like rays of the sun. "I know you understand how much I love you and how much Joe loves you. But as much as that is, God loves you even more. Trust Him to show you. Trust Him to provide the strength you so desperately need to keep going. You have God *within* you. Not just near or around you, within you." When she spoke of God, it was as if she was in another world, another place entirely. Like she truly understood how it felt to be in His presence.

"God walks on water, and He calms storms. He heals the sick and the brokenhearted. His unending, overwhelming love is stronger than any external force that could ever threaten us. Keep His words in your heart, Sunshine. The reward for your faith will be the peace you long for."

She gently lifted her hand from Sophia's head, placing it on the bare skin of her back. Her hand, once wrinkled and spotted with signs of its age, appeared refreshed, renewed somehow.

"I definitely need Him to calm this storm," I whispered.

"Oh, He will. Persevere in prayer, Sunshine, and He will direct your paths."

I knew there was a long road ahead of me. Though I prayed I would be able to look back on this all one day and share with others how God had used Sophia to conquer death, a hint of doubt still clung to my heart.

AN UNEXPECTED GIFT

I t was decided.

Sophia's surgery was set for ten in the morning the following day. She would be four days old. I hunkered down on the edge of the vinyl couch, staring at my surroundings. The room I now shared with my newborn daughter was small, nothing like the expansive window-walled space from Lillian's stay.

I thought then of Lillian. Guilt crept into my heart. Engulfed with Sophia's illness, I'd barely seen my firstborn in days. And even when I did, for brief moments of time, I found myself unable to focus on her the way I knew I should. My heart was continuously drawn to my second child, fighting for her life in the confines of a tiny hospital room. Other mothers had felt this way before me. I'd seen it in my own practice. It wasn't a conscious choice. It wasn't that we loved our other children any less. Our energy just became focused on the survival of the child who struggled to survive. I knew Lillian was safe, lovingly protected, and doted on by Joe's parents, and that brought me the security that allowed me to focus on Sophia. But I longed for a day when I would hold them both in my arms, their faces full of dimples and laughter.

The lights in the room were kept low to promote an environment of healing. But for me, the dimly lit, narrow room created more anxiety than healing. A million questions filtered through my mind, finding every crevasse and filling every gap. Every thought circled back to what could be.

"You look deep in thought over there." Mom's voice, though gentle, startled me out of my trance. Clutching my chest, I looked for her. I found her seated near me in the chair. *I could have sworn she wasn't here a minute ago. I must be going crazy.*

"Mom, you scared the crap out of me."

"Sonya, we don't say crap. Besides, I didn't mean to. You get that concentrated look on your face, and I swear your eyes turn darker."

"Mom, we don't swear," I smirked at my rebuttal as she rolled her eyes. "And I was deep in thought. I have so many unanswered questions, and my medical mind is running on overdrive."

It was the curse of the medical profession. When you or a loved one was sick, you often assumed the worst. And as usual, I'd allowed my mind to wander straight down the rabbit's hole of the unknown.

"You haven't been Googling again, have you?" She asked, remembering my epic breakdown following Sophia's birth in which Dr. Devi threatened to disconnect the Wi-Fi.

"No. Charley came by today. He explained what he remembered of CPAM from his general surgery days. He gave me some good questions to ask Dr. Devi and Dr. Holloway."

It was hard to believe it's only been days since I last saw him in the operating room. As closely as we'd worked all these years, I could tell he was happy to help in some way, even if it was just a listening ear or surgical knowledge.

"That was nice of him. Did he tell you anything important?"

In my heart, I knew it wasn't what he'd said but his demeanor that rattled me. Spending most of my waking hours working directly with him, I'd learned to recognize the meaning of his expressions. I noticed the look of sympathy in his eyes and understood the meaning behind his softened voice. He instinctively began to run his first finger along the nail of his thumb, a groove apparent from years' of wear. Though he wouldn't speak it to me, he was as concerned for Sophia as any surgeon would be.

"Yoo-hoo, Earth to Sonya." Mom waved her hand gently in front of my eyes, snapping me from my thoughts. I jolted back, eyes wide with attention.

"Sorry, got lost for a moment there. He didn't say too much. Our conversation did remind me that I wanted to call one of the anesthesiologists,

Dr. Davis. He works with a lot of the same kids that Charley and I do. He's experienced, and I trust him explicitly. I'm just waiting for a return text with his phone number.

As if on cue, my phone chirped. My heart sank as I read the message on the screen. "Here is his number, but he's on vacation. Want me to find you another one?" *No, I don't want you to find me another number. I wanted Dr. Davis.*

My thumbs punched at the phone, "I'll let you know." Despite the news, something within me stirred to call him. I knew he would answer my questions honestly, even if they weren't exactly what I wanted to hear.

I moved toward Sophia's open crib. "Momma will be right back. I'd move heaven and earth for you, my little sunshine."

Smiling at Mom, I strode to the door. "Can't explain now, but I'll be right back. Stay with Sophia, okay?"

I didn't give her a chance to respond and exited, closing the door softly behind me. Tapping the numbers into my phone, I waited anxiously while it rang.

"Hello?" Dr. Davis's voice projected through the other line.

"Hello, Dr. Davis?" Nervousness gripped me. *Get it together, Sonya.* I'd spoken to him countless times before, even engaging in lengthy conversations. But something about being on the other side made it all distinctly unfamiliar.

"Yes. Who is this?"

I slapped my hand to my forehead, hoping to knock in some sense.

"I'm sorry, Dr. Davis. This is Sonya Mack, from the OR. I was hoping you had a moment for a couple of questions. I know you're on vacation, and I'm so sorry to bother you, but I could really use your expertise." I pinched my nose hard and willed the tears to retreat until I was finished.

"Sonya," recognition in his voice. "You didn't sound like yourself. What can I do for you?"

That's because I'm not myself.

I told him the whole story, with every fact I knew, including her impending surgery tomorrow morning. Not often the quiet type, he listened silently except for a few quick sounds of understanding. When I finished my story, we discussed the risks, especially from his vantage point. He reassured me that she was in the hands of two talented surgeons.

"I know. I feel so very blessed to be acquainted with so many skilled doctors. I was going to see if you would be willing to do her anesthesia, but I know you're on vacation. Who do you think I should ask? There are so many good ones."

"Actually, I'm not leaving on my vacation for two more days. So if they are doing it tomorrow, I'll come in and do her case if you'd like."

Stunned, I forgot to speak. *Did I hear correctly? Was he really offering to come in on his day off to help me—to help Sophia?*

Though I desperately wanted him to, I couldn't ask him to come in on his day off. "Dr. Davis, you don't need to." Before I could reason any further, he interrupted me.

"I insist," his voice was clear, definite, "as long as it's tomorrow."

My heart raced as I squinted to hold back my emotions. Staring into the blue sky, dotted with wisps of white clouds, I whispered, "Thank you, Lord."

I swallowed, attempting to choke back the shakiness in my voice.

"I would love that."

"Okay then, I'll be there in the morning to check her out. Try to get some rest. We'll take good care of her."

"I know you will, Dr. Davis. Thank you so much."

The phone clicked, ending the call. I couldn't help but smile through a flood of emotions. A sudden blanket of peace began to wrap its way around my body. For the first time in days, I was beginning to feel the weight of fear lift, even if for just a moment.

IT'S TIME

We sat soundlessly, watching each second tick away on the clock. Minutes felt like hours, yet passed too quickly as we waited for the nurses to take Sophia to surgery.

Curling my hand around her, I felt the rise and fall with each puff of the ventilator. There was nothing more I could do. I had assembled the best team of doctors and knew the rest of Sophia's story would be placed right where it belonged—in God's hands. I imagined her there, nestled in the strong, gentle hands of our Father as he whispered, "My dear child, I have knitted you together in your mother's womb. I know the plans I have for your future and those of your parents. Plans, not of harm, but hope. Plans to fill your life with good things. You will be strong like an eagle. I will never leave your side, sweet Sophia. Rest safely in my arms, sweet child."

I traced each part of her, memorizing every curve of her face from her chubby soft cheeks to her tiny button nose. Each finger, miniature but perfect, was imprinted in my memory. Not knowing if I would ever hold her like this again, I was desperate to remember every inch of her. Through blurry eyes, I noticed Mom and Joe join me around her crib.

The nurse knocked gently on the door and opened it without a word. Behind her stood more nurses I recognized in familiar green scrubs. "It's time."

Stepping back from Sophia's crib, I studied them as they worked meticulously to transfer her wire-strung body to the mobile transport incubator. I winced against the pain building in me.

I felt Mom's hand grasp mine. "She's in God's hands now."

Before leaving the room, I quickly grabbed the precious family quilt, knowing the prayers of those who had fashioned it lay within each stitch. Once Sophia was settled into the isolette, we began our slow course to the OR. Mom stayed behind, recognizing this was a moment for Joe and me. We shuffled our weakened bodies behind the crowd of nurses, hands linked in the comfort of one another. I couldn't help but notice all the smiling faces and jolly voices of those around me. I thought briefly at the irony of the situation. While bystanders enjoyed a normal, uneventful day, I stood at the juncture that would define my child's entire future—a fork in the road, and I could never turn back.

As we neared the big metal doors that would lead us into the OR, I recognized the large red line painted into the floor ahead. The nurses slowed their pace. One turned to look at me. Her eyes were kind, sympathetic. "This is where we go on alone. Would you like to kiss her first?"

I nodded my head, knowing words would fracture me. Moving toward Sophia, I raised the plexiglass panel on the side of the transporter. I touched my lips to her cheek. Her heat felt like electricity. "Mommy and Daddy love you so much, baby. I can't go in there with you, but God will be holding you the whole time. Until we meet again, be strong little one."

I stepped back, allowing Joe to have his last moment with her. Placing his hand on her head, cradling it gently, he bent down, touching his lips to her forehead. As he stepped back toward me, I noticed his film of tears. Together we watched as they wheeled on farther down the hall, a piece of us in the little cart they were pushing. I stood motionless until the final metal door closed, blocking her from my view. I knew where I was supposed to go. I knew my feet should move me to the waiting room just down the hall, but I was frozen. "What if that's the last time I see her?" I wanted to be strong and have faith, but I couldn't stop the thought from entering my mind. Fear seized me to the pale tiled floor. No longer could I hold back the flood of emotions. I wasn't composed. I was broken. I clutched my quilt, tears like sheets of rain, splashed to the ground. Joe's strong arm wrapped around the curve of my back. I sank into him.

"It's God's plan, Sonya." My rock and my strength, his words medicinal to my fragile soul.

Standing up taller, I wiped the wetness from my cheeks. A peace, like the smallest flicker of a candle lighting up a dark room, began to fill my soul, pulsing outward.

"You're right, Joe. This is God's plan."

IT IS DONE

I was forever changed that day. I no longer lived each predictable day as it morphed into the next. Life was precious, not meant to be lived simply, but a gift to be grateful for every single day.

Sitting in the crowded waiting room for more than two hours, I watched the meanderings of families waiting for doctors to appear from behind the door that led into the recovery room. I wondered as I peered at each of their faces, would their life be forever changed as mine would?

Sensing my internal struggle, Mom reached for my hand. Her presence filled the space within me that felt hollow. I nuzzled my head onto her shoulder, allowing myself for a moment to forget my baby was fighting for her life.

She whispered next to my ear. "You know, I've always admired how strong you are."

"I don't feel very strong right now. All I ever wanted was a healthy baby. But what does that even mean? If a baby is born early and spends weeks in the NICU, but goes home as if it were born to term, is that a healthy baby? Or what about a baby born with a serious condition that is treated or fixed? Is that healthy? What if your baby isn't born healthy? Why do I have two children who were both born needing serious medical treatment, but others have four, five, or even more born without any issues? And what about the babies that never get to come home? How is that fair?"

She squeezed gently on my shoulder. "Sweetheart, life isn't about fairness. It's about taking what we have been given and using that experience to better ourselves and others. You have already endured so much and come out on the other side stronger and more prepared for a world full of the unexpected. Someday you will be able to share your story, and it will change the lives of so many people. Today isn't about focusing on what's fair. I know that may sound harsh, but it isn't meant to be. Today and every day are about putting your mind and heart in a place of gratitude. There is joy in the journey, Sonya. Someday, you will see this all play together like a beautiful symphony. But right now, you have to trust God to be the Grand Conductor."

Her words sparked a memory within me. I had already endured an event so indescribably life-changing. Yet, rather than let it wither me away in grief and fear, I chose instead to use it as a catalyst to change my life, to rewrite my own story. Sophia's story would be like that, another obstacle on the road of life serving as an impetus for something unforgettable.

I contemplated the events of the last few years of my life. Often after traversing to the other side of my most difficult struggles, I was able to recognize these moments as the life-changing lessons they were. No matter what the future held for Sophia, her story, too, would be an impetus for something life-altering.

As I stared forward, deep in thought, I noticed the nurse liaison walking toward me. I knew her well as she came in the OR often to check on the patients, relaying the message to anxiously-waiting family members. She was a short, older woman who had an infectious smile. She was perfect for the job.

"The surgery is finished. They would like to meet you in a consult room."

Though her smiling face made me want to believe everything had gone well, the consult rooms were usually reserved for more serious conversations. My heart was heavy with anxious tension as I gathered my things. Even if I asked, she would want me to hear the results from the doctor. The three of us hurried into the square room. A small table sat in the center, surrounded by four chairs. A whiteboard hung on the wall.

I sat down silently in one of the chairs, Joe next to me while Mom stood in the corner. The door opened on the opposite side of the room, and fear spasmed me. The doctors' next words would determine the trajectory of my life.

I examined their faces for any warning signs of the news to come, a hint of sadness or a glint of hope. My survey revealed nothing. True champions in their fields, they remained stalwart in emotion as they sat down at the table. Questions raced through me. If everything went well, why weren't they saying anything? Why weren't they smiling? What happened to my baby? Dear God, please tell me my baby is safe. You told me Yourself everything would be okay.

After glancing at me, Dr. Devi looked toward Dr. Holloway. I knew the gesture meant Dr. Holloway had performed more of the surgery than anticipated. My heart skipped in anxious anticipation.

A reserved man, Dr. Holloway carried himself without a deluge of emotion. Though only moments before he spoke, it felt like a lifetime to my heart. "The surgery went well. She's stable and on her way back up to get settled in."

The pressure building within me released slightly. Though I knew his report should fill me with resounding joy, there was something he left unsaid. Perhaps it was the quiet reverence in his voice that most surgeons used when there was more information to come. I'd worked with enough surgeons to know they sometimes gave the good news first, to soften the blow of any devastating results. I started to speak but stopped.

He continued, his eyes direct and voice assured. "We were able to get the whole cyst out. It was impressive, but Dr. Davis was able to ventilate her with just one lung, so it made the process much more direct."

I whispered a silent prayer of gratitude for Dr. Davis and smiled softly. In my heart, I knew there was still more. Despite the positive news which should have filled the room with ecstatic waves of joy, there remained a hint of reservation in his voice.

There was still the question of whether her remaining lung tissue was healthy, just collapsed under the weight of the cyst. I needed to ask the question and steeled myself for the answer.

"Dr. Holloway, how are the rest of her lungs? Did they inflate? Will she be able to breathe on her own?"

His eyes appeared to darken with the weight of my question. There was always an intense internal struggle to relay unfavorable information. I sensed he was phrasing his words carefully to relay correct information without undue worry.

After a few moments, he cleared his voice. "When we removed the cyst, the left lung fully inflated. However, the right lung did not completely fill the cavity the mass had occupied. Though we are optimistic, right now, we can't be exactly sure what the capacity of her right lung will be."

For the first time in four days, I took a deep, satisfying breath. The news wasn't perfect. He didn't say everything was just as they'd hoped, but I could read between the lines. I felt the optimism in his voice and recognized the hope in his features. There was still some uncertainty, but in the course of a marathon, we were nearing the race's final leg. My baby was alive. She had survived to breathe another day. Some parents and families would not be granted the same gift today. Somewhere out there, a mother and father were grieving the loss of their infant, enduring unimaginable heartache and pain. At the same time, Joe and I were avowed another day. My heart ached for them.

Joe and I stood from our chairs. Though I wanted to run to them, arms wide, and encircle them both, I opted instead to reach out my hand. Dr. Holloway grasped mine, and I squeezed tightly. I prayed all the gratitude, every ounce of thanks I felt within my heart, would be transferred in one single handshake. "Thank you." I looked from Dr. Holloway to Dr. Devi. "Thank you for saving our baby girl."

"You're welcome." Dr. Holloway's voice was soft. Despite his usual reserved status, I witnessed a glimmer of a smile on his face. "We'll check in on you tomorrow. Why don't you go up and see your baby."

"I will. Thank you so much, doctors. I could never express in words how deeply I appreciate your expertise. Thank you for saving my daughter." My heart rolled in a quiver of emotion. I recognized there was still a degree of the unknown. God had been faithful to His word, and I would continue to trust in that reality.

Dr. Devi began toward the door with a gentle grin and a wave, followed by Dr. Holloway. Shifting toward Joe, I hugged him with desperate intensity. "She's alive."

He buried his face into my hair. I thought I heard him sniff, overcome with emotion, but I would let him hide his emotion. We sat silently for a moment, processing all the emotions of the last few days. In the depths of my thought, it was Mom who broke our silence.

"How are you feeling, Sunshine?"

Her voice, gentle as always, served as a magnet to bring me back into the present. I pondered her question. How was I doing? I imagined myself on a roller coaster. In the last four days, I'd ridden a wave of emotions. From the euphoria of giving birth to the devastation of not knowing if my child would survive, I'd endured more than some parents would in an entire lifetime. Looking back now, peering into the past with the realization of the future, I was filled with a renewed sense of optimism, a revitalized feeling of hope.

"Well, Mom. I'm doing well. I know there are still some unknowns lingering in the distance, but God has proven His magnificence."

Trying hard to encircle both Joe and me in her short arms, she snuggled into us. "Let's go see your baby."

As we walked toward the NICU, hope filled my being. There is a quiet beauty in its symbolism. Hope reaches the deepest parts of us, even when faith is shallow, and optimism fades. I would rely on that hope to lift me up and give me the ability to fight, survive, and live one more day. Hope in the Lord, that was our future.

FINALLY HOME

I cursed the phone as it blared on the wall, interrupting my quiet reflection. I finally had a moment to settle into my favorite recliner, wrapped in the familiar warmth of home.

"Hello?" My voice was curt, frustrated with the caller on the other end.

"Sonya?" I recognized Mom's voice instantly, her tone remorseful, probably due to my greeting.

"Oh, hi, Mom." I regretted my outburst. It'd been two weeks since we'd brought Sophia home from the hospital. The entire ordeal was still sharp in my mind. Though the doctors remained unsure of her lung development at first, true to His word, God breathed life and fullness into her lungs. There would, undoubtedly, be multiple appointments to follow, but only a mere two days after Sophia's surgery, they removed the ventilator. No longer under the haze of sedatives and pain medications, I was able to look into her eyes for the first time since she was born. A brilliant deep blue, I nearly drowned in their depth.

Two weeks following her birth, we packed up and left for home, despite a mountain of uncertainty and life-altering surgery.

"I'm so sorry, Sunshine, did I interrupt you? I just wanted to check in and see how everyone was doing?"

"No, Mom. I'm sorry if I sounded curt. I just got Sophia and Lillian down for a nap and didn't want the phone to wake them. They're still sleeping, though. I was ready to curse out a telemarketer if necessary."

"Thank goodness I'm not one of them, or I might have to cover my ears." I heard her familiar cackle on the other end. Her uncanny ability to elicit joy in those around her never ceased to amaze me.

"Good thing." I smiled despite myself.

"Anyway, I was just calling to see how things were going now that you've been home for a few days."

"Well . . ." The word drew out in recognition of all I'd endured in such a short period of time. "I am finding motherhood a complete mix of emotions. Most days, I love my children more than anything. Their sweet kisses and precious sleeping faces fill my heart with so much joy, I'm afraid it may burst. But I wonder sometimes—do all moms have moments when they question, even just for an instant, if they were meant to be just that—mothers? What do you do when the sleepless nights, the whining, temper tantrums, and every hardship of parenting begin to weigh you down?" I was ashamed to ask, but with weakness, sleep deprivation, and hormones coursing through me, I was exhausted. Like an addict, I'd been riding the high of Sophia's story of redemption and survival. In its wake, in the reality and responsibility of being at home, the burden of parenthood began to overwhelm me.

"I know it sounds terrible. I just feel so overwhelmed right now. Sophia's home, and I'm so incredibly and undeniably grateful. But my heart is heavy with what remains in the wake of her illness. One specialist leads to another and another: pulmonology, Ear Nose and Throat, Cardiology, Gastroenterology, and a developmental clinic. Almost every part of her body has a specialist! As if that isn't enough, each requires a different set of testing. In the midst of all the insanity, I see her innocent, tiny face, and all I want to do is protect her. And then, the struggle starts again."

There was silence on the other end of the line. Afraid my comments might finally be the one realization that caused my mother to be disappointed in me, I opened my mouth to speak. I wanted to tell her I was joking. Of course, I was made for motherhood. These were just silly emotions instigated by a flurry of postpartum hormones and sleep deprivation. Before I could defend myself, she spoke.

"Oh, Sonya. The Lord knows every mother has felt this way at some moment in her life." A forceful laugh followed by a snort blared through the phone. "In fact, there was a point with you kids when it seemed all you could do was fight with each other. I dropped you off with your grandma and thought about leaving you there." The memory must have tickled her funny bone because she laughed with such intensity that I could hear her gulp for air.

Her raucous, jubilant laughter was infectious. Each subsequent chuckle reproduced between us until tears cascaded down my face. It was minutes before we began to settle down. I wiped the evidence from my face and smiled as I acknowledged the ache in my stomach. "Wow, I haven't used those muscles in a while."

It took me a moment to catch my breath. "Goodness, Mom. I nearly wet my pants! You shouldn't make women who just had a baby laugh so hard. I'm fairly certain that was the most work my abs have seen in months."

"Well, it sounded to me like you needed it. Wet panties and all." Her tinkled laugh blurted out once more. "But in all seriousness, Sunshine, every mother has felt that way. There are moments you love your children so much, you would die for them, but seconds later, you want to permanently drop them off at Grandma's." She paused, and I sensed she was collecting her thoughts on the other end.

"Motherhood was the most difficult and equally rewarding experience of my life. I am confident it will be yours, as well. It's an eternal rollercoaster ride. Being a Mom is beautiful and magical, but it's also chaotic and messy. There will be days when you rock it like that long-haired guy from Aerosmith, and other days you feel nothing is going right. But at the end of every day, when you peer in on their sweet sleeping faces, you'll be reminded why it was all worth it.

"Give yourself a break, Sonya. You've just walked through hell. You are mentally and physically exhausted. I promise you, someday, God will use this experience to create something unimaginable, and you will find your flow in the realm of motherhood."

I clicked the big silver button on the top of the baby monitor. Before Sophia was born, we'd upgraded to the two-camera model. I looked at the silhouettes of my sleeping babies with love. "You're right. I'm just walking through a valley right now, but someday, I'll be back up on the mountain, and it will all seem more clear. Thank you for being a voice of reason in my chaos."

"Sunshine, you know I am always, *always* here for you. Nothing could ever separate you from my love." Even though she wasn't physically near me, I could still see the deep dimples in her soft round cheeks, and her smile spread across her face flanked by locks of auburn hair.

"I guess that was a really long answer to your question of how we were doing, huh?"

"Yes, but sometimes, that's what we need."

I nodded in acknowledgment. A good conversation with Mom had been the cure for most of what ailed me throughout the years.

"When you called, I was actually just reminiscing about the incredible way every detail seemed to weave together regarding Sophia's birth. I still find it hard to believe how quickly she recovered after her surgery. I mean, can you believe it was only ten days after having an entire lobe of her lung removed that we were able to take her home with no oxygen or pain medications? When I take a moment to remind myself how beautifully it was orchestrated, I'm overwhelmed."

"Overwhelmed, like the view from the mountaintop, is a good place to be."

"A view from the mountaintops." I thought about how long it'd been since we'd sat on those horses in Colorado overlooking the expansive terrain of the Rocky Mountains. "Speaking of awe and mountaintops. Aren't we due for another adventure? I know I can't go *right* now, but we should plan something for a few months from now after Sophia's appointments calm down. What do you think?"

"That sounds incredible." She eeked. "I wouldn't even begin to know where to go. Just not that Las Vegas place. I don't think I would do well in Sin City. It would probably eat me alive."

Even the thought of my tiny naive mother in the whirlwind of Las Vegas filled me with angst, as I remembered nearly losing her in the Orland airport. The bizarre atmosphere of Sin City might swallow her up.

"I think you're right, Mom. Maybe something a little less crazy. I've always wanted to go to the Northeast. What about somewhere like Vermont or New Hampshire? A friend of mine told me it's beautiful there, lots of parks, forests, and history."

"You tell me when and where, and I'll be there."

"It's a date. It'll probably be a few months, but I already can't wait."

The monitor blared as Sophia's cry interrupted our conversation. "I have to go because the baby's crying, but…" I would never be able to fully articulate how much her love encompassed everything I longed to be as a mother. I knew at that moment, I would spend my life telling her and anyone who would listen how deeply her love molded me into who I had become. "Mom?"

"What is it, sweetheart? Is everything all right?" Mom recognized the somber, reflective tone in my voice.

"Nothing's the matter. I just need you to know how much I love you and how insanely I miss you when you're gone. Thank you for always being there for me, even when you can't be here physically. Seems no matter how old I get, I always need my mom."

"Sunshine, you know the bond of motherhood can never be severed. Time, space, distance—nothing will ever separate us. I am always in your heart. Find me there, whenever you need me. Now. Go get that precious baby, and snuggle her tight for me. I'll see you again soon, maybe when we're standing on the top of a mountain."

MOUNTAIN TOP

"I'm not going to make it." Mom paused, staring up at the tall structure. "I can't do this, Sonya. It's too much. I'll never make it." Her words were breathless, nearly whispers as we reached the final few steps.

"I know it's hard, but you can make it. You only have a little farther to go. I promise the reward for the entire struggle and hard work is always worth the fight in the end." I stopped climbing and waited for her to catch her breath. The view around us left me speechless.

We were nearing the end of our 158 step climb to the top of the Harris Hill Ski Jump in Brattleboro, Vermont. We'd originally planned a trip to Boston for historical purposes but the highly-treed, rolling, mountainous landscape of the surrounding New England states drew us away from the urban scene into the more quiet scenery of the inland states. We drove west from Massachusetts and happened upon Brattleboro as we crossed from New Hampshire into Vermont. Nestled into the hills adjacent to the Connecticut River, the quiet, historic charm lured our attention.

Earlier, we'd stopped by a local dairy market to purchase various cheeses, meats, and jellies. Finding a small park with plenty of big, lush trees, we settled into a picnic table to eat a quick lunch. Traffic flowed smoothly around the square as we relished the quiet environment. We stayed for a while chatting easily before we decided to drive around the town.

Rising out of the mass of the luscious fall foliage was a towering wooden structure. Curiosity struck me as I pulled onto the dirt road that led down the grassy area I assumed was for parking. The car bumped hard along the rough ground as I drove closer to the structure's base.

"What is that thing anyway?" Mom's eyes widened.

"It's a ski jump. You know, like in the Olympics."

"You mean the ones where they lean *way* forward and then jump off the end?" She made a scooping motion with her hand, mimicking the athlete's trajectory.

"That's what it looks like." I stopped the car near the base of the hill. Putting the car in park, I opened my door into the warm breeze. It was a radiant early fall day. The sun beamed down in rods reflected from Heaven. The wind gently brought the earthy smell of the river that lay to the east.

Stepping out into the sunshine, I turned in a complete circle surveying the scene. Thick forest surrounded the ski jump, jutting up toward the sky. Steps lined the structure on either side, though only one side reached the top. The large grassy area where we stood created a circular area with dense forest on all sides. It was silent, nearly secluded from the surrounding town. The only sound was the soft hum of nearby traffic on the road we'd exited.

"Isn't this amazing? I bet we can see for miles up there." I turned to Mom. Her face was full of angst. She appeared to be struggling with something internally. "Mom?" She didn't answer, still lost in her thoughts.

"Mom!" I yelled, jerking her out of her trance.

"Huh." She jumped back, startled. She scoped out the scene in front of her. "That's a long way up. You aren't expecting me to climb that are you? Because there is no way I am doing that."

I walked around the car and put my arm around her back. "But imagine how beautiful it will be up there. You can't possibly be afraid of heights anymore. But even if you were, it'll be worth it. I'll be right next to you, guiding you to the top."

She scanned the structure once more, closing her eyes. I could only imagine what she might be saying. "Dear Lord, I don't think I could fall to my death, but either way, please keep us safe. Give me the strength to climb those steps to the top. Love, Vicki."

The precious, gentle way she bowed her head and shut her eyes tight in reverence made me smile with radiant joy. She was closer to God than anyone I knew, intimately, in a way I could not yet fully understand.

She nodded silently as if hearing the audible answer to her prayer. Turning back to me, she flashed me her most adventurous smile. "Okay, Sunshine, I'm ready. Let's climb that mountain."

Before she could change her mind, I seized her hand and hiked toward the gate that led to the stairs.

*****

Finally at the top of the structure, we perched ourselves on a bench that traversed the distance. Miles of rolling amber and fire leaves spotted with verdant trees yet to change stretched before us. Tiny houses dotted the landscape connected by roads like strands of gray twine. I breathed the fresh autumn air deeply, I'd never felt closer to God. Perhaps it was the height, the proximity to heaven, or the stillness of life at this level, but as I gazed in wonderment, my life was forever changed.

Mom turned her face into its warmth, her lips moving in silent gratitude. I stared, unable to release my eyes from her. There was magic in the effortless way she communicated with God. I understood her connection. She was closer to Him, knew Him more intimately than I could physically fathom. The realization, I, too, would someday know Him so intimately filled me with an awe I could not explain. I sank into the gloriousness of the moment. She opened her eyes, noticing my tears.

"What's wrong, Sunshine?"

"It's so beautiful up here. I've been struggling with so much lately. Not just the girls and motherhood, but an intense internal feeling that I'm meant to do something different, something bigger than I could imagine with my life. It sounds crazy when I say it out loud. I have a successful career with people who appreciate me. I help change lives every day, and I know that's impactful. But there's a deeper pull that runs through my veins. I've prayed about it for so long, even tried to bury it, thinking at first it was a fluke feeling of ego. But it won't go away. No matter how hard I try. I'm afraid if I continue to try and suffocate it, I will be the one who ends up smothered.

She listened intently. Only when I paused, staring off into the landscape, she spoke.

"For a while now, I've felt that you were struggling with something deep, but just assumed it was still everything you went through with Sophia and me."

Staring into the expanse of trees, the leaves rolled like waves on the ocean's surface. I was transfixed by the beauty of the changing landscape, reminiscent of what was within my own heart. It was difficult to recall the exact point when I realized I could no longer stay peacefully where I was in the warm, gentle waters of a career I knew so well. Instead, I knew that I must venture into the deeper, much colder waters of the unknown.

"I can't say for sure when the feeling started. If I thought about it, I'd say probably when we were going through your illness." She nodded sympathetically, understanding the great burden her illness had placed on us all. "It was such a difficult and intensely life-changing time. I was sure the feeling arose out of the struggle. I assumed once it was all over and we'd begun to adjust to our new normal, I'd find solace in the reliability of the familiar. But I never did. It didn't matter how much I prayed to bury it or ignore it. God continued to bring me back to this new calling." I shrugged, still not fully aware of what I was sensing.

She reached for my hand, gripping it tightly. "I'm so sorry you're dealing with this, Sunshine, especially if I caused any part of it."

I was about to interrupt, to clarify it was never her fault, but she placed a finger on her lips to stop my comments.

She breathed in sharply, closing her eyes in the warmth of the soft sunshine. "I struggled so much with my illness. Not just the fear and heartache I had over everything I was losing, but most importantly, how it was impacting all of you. I recognized the desperation and fear on your faces, even though you never shared it outwardly. Your tired eyes and weary faces told of the emotions you never would. Your hearts were breaking just like mine, but we were powerless to change it.

"I've learned so much in the years since. I've seen how God uses these deep internal struggles as a way of speaking to us. As a way to stir our hearts into digging deeper within ourselves to follow a calling we may not have previously been ready, or willing, to understand. He has a plan to weave every experience into our ultimate calling. I could never fully explain the unbelievable way that He quilts together our lives. It will make more sense to you someday. For now, you'll have to believe me. Don't ever let go of this feeling within. You must keep following it.

Her hand rose to my cheek, giving it a gentle pat. "What do you feel He's calling you to do?"

I turned away, embarrassed to acknowledge my thoughts. A quick laugh escaped me, still denying my call internally.

In the distance, blackbirds cascaded in a blanket of onyx, seamlessly weaving to the rhythm and pattern of their leader. I longed for the simplicity of their following, to know exactly where to go without question. The words I spoke next rushed from my lips, afraid if I didn't release it now, I might never.

"I want to be a writer, or an author, or a speaker. Maybe one of them. Or all of them. I don't know. All I know is lately, I've carried a heavy unshakeable sense to write a book. Many books, actually. You know how much I've found solace in writing since I was young. But I've never had any training except for a couple of lame college courses. I stay awake at night, dreaming about writing books and sharing my story. I long to help others navigate whatever difficulty they may face by sharing what I've already lived through, showing them a new way to heal. It fills me with so much joy to think about. Sometimes I'm afraid I might burst."

"But I don't know what I'm doing, and it's such a tough industry to get into. Maybe I'm crazy. But I do know, when I think about not doing it, when I think about giving up," I trailed off.

Wetness blurred my sight, creating a kaleidoscope of colors around me. This calling had been bubbling within me for years, but I'd always hidden it for fear of the unknown. Fear that if I started to let it out, the magnitude of chasing it might ruin me. But what I'd realized instead was in my attempt to bury it, I was suffocating in silence. Heavy tears, weighted by years of longing and secrecy, spilled out over my cheeks.

"Sunshine," Her voice was as soft as the gentle autumn breeze on my cheeks. "I know any vocation is difficult, but most importantly, there is joy in the journey. There is a joy in knowing that our Heavenly Father has perfectly planned these opportunities for us to learn and grow in love and patience. There is joy in knowing we can truly bless others in the future.

"You have always been in such a hurry to get where you're going. You decide you want something and you go after it. I've always admired your determination, except when you get impatient. You want it on your time, not God's. Though it's important to focus on the end goal, it's even more important to recognize the significance of the journey. There is molding, learning, and shaping along the way."

She looked out into the expanse before us. "That's why I loved doing ceramics so much. When I first bought a piece, it was greenware—just clay with rough, raw edges that needed to be shaped. But I enjoyed the process of shaving off those edges and sponging them smooth. Even once all the edges were polished, they still had to endure intense heat and fire in the kiln before I could begin to paint them. Once fired, they came out solid and stronger, but still fragile. It was then that I could finally start adding the brilliant colors that would turn them into what their final product would be. Each layer of paint added a new dimension, a new layer of beauty.

"In the final steps, after a tremendous journey, they were ready to be sealed, keeping them protected from the elements. But no piece could ever become the colorful, strong, sealed version of itself without first enduring the molding and heat of the fire. There is great joy in the process, Sonya, for the artist and the masterpiece. To go from rough and unfinished to pretty and polished—it's magical.

"Look around you, Sunshine." She held her arms open to the vast beauty displayed before us. "Each and every one of these trees goes through intense changes each year. They'll have periods of elegance and vibrancy, but also endure times of barrenness and cold.

"Everything you've been through, my illness, Sophia's story, each heartbreak was there for a reason. Life is always changing, and we're always learning. The external elements can be harsh and threatening, trying to wear down our outer sealant, just like those ceramics. And, like them, we get knocked down and may even chip or break. But in the same way that I glued them back together, repainted the edges, and sealed them back up, God does that for us, too. No matter how the elements of our lives damage us in our journey, He is always there to put our pieces back together, to make us whole again."

With her hands on my shoulders, she kissed my forehead. She pulled me into a tight embrace, resting her head next to my ear. As if the conversation were private, meant just for us, she whispered the rest into my ear. "Enjoy the journey, Sunshine. Embrace the molding and shaping, the people you meet, the lessons you learn. Embrace it all. Keep following that feeling. Hold it tight in your heart, never believing, even for a second, that you aren't capable of every dream you hold there. If your dreams are for the betterment of you and others, God put them there. Follow those.

"I named you Sonya Joy for a reason. You were born to bring joy to others, and you will. I love you and the rest of the family more than anything in this entire universe. I want nothing more than your happiness. Don't forget to slow down now and again. Be still and know that He is God. He will get you there. I promise."

I inhaled her sweet fragrant scent allowing it to perfuse my veins. I held her tight, never sure when I would see her again. When I pulled back, her body was surrounded by a halo of golden sunlight, so bright her silhouette appeared to glow. I stared into the halo of light as she rose from her seat.

Kissing me one last time on the top of my head, she whispered. "I'm always here with you, Sunshine. Remember, not time, space, or death can keep me from you. You've kept me alive in your memories, and I'll always be with you in your heart. Because of that bond, created and forged by God, even though I can't be here physically, I can go anywhere with you. There is no place too far and no struggle too great you won't find me right here, in your heart, and your memories."

I knew our time was coming to an end as it always did. I longed to keep her here but knew it was no longer her home. My brother told me that her memories and our love will always keep her alive in my heart. I'd seen this evidence countless times—our trips to Colorado, Disney, and Mexico, and by my side when my children were born, just like I knew she would. Her illness and her death created a chasm in my soul so deep I thought I'd never recover, but her memory has kept her forever a part of my life.

She started down the steps, turning back to wave one final goodbye. Behind her, a small yellow butterfly fluttered gently in the breeze. Drawn to it, I stretched out my hand. As my fingers reached forward, her figure disappeared as quickly as it had arrived. In her absence was an emptiness I'd felt before. The tiny creature landed delicately upon my hand. Bringing it closer, I admired its beauty.

"I know you can't stay forever, Mom, but I need you to know how much I love you. I miss you so much I can't bear it sometimes. I know you're forever in my heart. Our bond will never be broken—not by time, not by space, not by death."

A gust of wind blew gently on my back, and with it, the butterfly fluttered off. "I love you, Mom. Until I see you again." My final kiss blew away with the fall breeze.

December 2010

THE END IS THE BEGINNING

Despite my longing to stay there, lying in my childhood home next to the woman who gave me life, it wasn't long before the rest of my family trickled out of rooms and up the stairs. Hushed voices filtered in from the kitchen, and I wondered what they were speaking of as if this were just another day.

The wind howled outside the sliding glass door, and swirls of snow whisked over the barren cornfields. Verdant cornstalks waved in unison, stretching for miles in the summer while red-winged blackbirds squawked to protect their nests. When harvest came and emptied the fields of their protective cover, the winter winds stopped for nothing and chilled us to the bone.

Kissing my mother's cheek, I rose from her bed and walked toward the door. Watching my breath spread across the glass, I pressed my finger into it. Enjoying the cold sensation, I traced three letters—ALS. Amyotrophic Lateral Sclerosis. The words still tasted like acid in my mouth. I cursed again the disease that had attacked her nerve cells, degenerating her muscles over time. Like a slow-burning candle, it had paralyzed her body—first her legs and arms, then her tongue, and finally, her breath. I recalled the words she spoke to me only days before. "I don't want to leave you all, but can you imagine how wonderful heaven will be?" ALS could steal her body, but it could not steal her faith.

A gentle knock at the back door broke my stare—the doctor's arrival a reminder of what little time we had left. I could hear my family's whispered "hellos" as he entered. Once the ventilator was removed, my mother's remaining time would be limited. Yet, the doctor's presence meant her transition from this life to one with Jesus would be pain-free. Though his degree had prepared him for this day, it couldn't hide his sadness. Tears veiled his eyes when they finally met mine as he twisted a syringe onto Mom's IV.

Something about the finality of my mother's condition and our inability to fight against it made me recognize I could never fully control my future. Like the snowflakes outside the window, I was at the mercy of a power far greater than my own smallness. The road to healing would be painful, but I understood, in the hands of God, the struggle is intentional.

Making his way toward the ventilator, the doctor positioned his finger on the power switch. He inhaled deeply before lifting his gaze to meet mine. For months he had visited my mother here, in her home, taking time from his busy schedule to make house calls in a day when they were considered a luxury of the past. His presence today meant Mom's transition from a life supported by machines to one with Jesus would be pain-free. With a final nod in my direction and a click that shattered my existence, the ventilator went silent. Once the process started, I knew that seeing her last breath would be more than I could endure.

I leaned down and nestled my head next to hers, my voice in her ear. "Everything's going to be all right, Mom. You're free now. No more disease. No more pain. Please don't worry about me. I'll take you with me wherever I go—mountaintops, seashores, when my babies are born, just like we've imagined it, you'll be there." The interval between her breaths lengthened, each one closer to her last. "I know we'll always have a guardian angel. Your spirit will go with us. I'll see you in the butterflies, just like you promised. I'll never forget your laughter, your love, or your faith. You can go now; go be with Jesus." She inhaled weakly, one last time, and with her final breath, I began to sing "You are My Sunshine," the words hushed through my sobs.

The quiet sniffs of my family filled the room as I laid my ear to her chest. Her heartbeats, slowing, getting farther and farther apart as if traveling away from me until they were gone. With the final beat of her heart, my soul cracked down its center.

ALIVE IN MY MEMORIES

"Eek," a high-pitched shriek from Sophia, my two-year-old, shook me, drawing me out of my memory. Streaking past me naked as the day she was born, her blonde ringlets reflected the Christmas lights as she dodged the tree on her way to join the others in my aunt's kitchen. She giggled as her older sister, Lillian, chased her, a sound that used to make me smile, but not today. Today, I turned only long enough to catch the faintest hint of the scar that traversed the right side of her back. The thin line acted as a reminder of how we almost lost her, too. I shuddered at the memory.

I thought about joining the others, telling the kids to calm down or stop running in the house, or insisting Sophia wear her clothes. After all, it was Christmas Eve, but Joe would eventually realize what was happening and corral them. Guilt rose up as I contemplated my apathy, but I didn't have the energy to move. Honestly, I didn't care. I'd become a shell of myself.

My family always gathered at Christmastime. The kitchen of my aunt's house was full of my family members catching up on old memories. It used to be my favorite time of year, but it wasn't the same anymore, not without Mom's effervescent laughter. It was hard to believe that so much time had passed. My body still ached with grief that settled in my bones like metastatic cancer with no offer of treatment. To say I loved my mother seems somehow superficial. In many ways, she was more than a mother. She was my center; the sun most of my life orbited around. Without the sun, there was only darkness.

I swiped at my eyes to remove the remaining tears. My hand gripped my shirt, surprised the events of that day still caused such physical pain.

In the kitchen, my brother Shane stood in the center of my extended family. Though I couldn't hear his words, I knew he was telling a story by the way his eyes crinkled mischievously at the edges. Aunt Tina, Uncle Rich, and my sister Wendy sat nearby, all smiles and attentive eyes. It's hard to believe how much Wendy looked like Mom with her round cheeks and red hair that lightened every year.

Shane's tall, fit frame and eloquent speech always had a way of commanding attention. Seven years my elder, his copper hair had begun to thin at the back. I couldn't help but grin. Only after reaching adulthood had he taken on the role of the protective older brother. His background in psychology and ability to listen without judgment made him the perfect sounding board. I missed him and wondered why I didn't call him more.

As usual, my father sat in the corner, munching on the candies my aunt made. He'd gained a little weight since he left, his belly spilling further onto his lap. He'd moved to Albuquerque after Mom died, but I knew he was happy there in the desert solitude. We'd never been very close. Though I respected the backbreaking work he'd endured to provide for our family and the gentle way he cared for Mom, my admiration for him was mostly from afar. During my childhood, snuggles with my father were often met with resistance, as if he wasn't quite sure what to do with me. I didn't blame him. He only mirrored the response of his own parents—understood love and provision, but without much in the way of affection. Yet, after Mom died, there seemed to be a softer side of Dad I'd never seen before.

When a screech from one of my children diverted Shane's eyes, he scanned the room for the source of the noise and noticed me staring. He tilted his head and mouthed, "You okay?"

I shrugged. *Was I?*

As he walked toward me, I could feel tears forming. Was I ready for this? It was easy to ignore him and tell him everything was fine when he lived three states away. But, with him next to me, would I still be able to pretend? He always seemed to know when I was lying.

Plopping down beside me, he asked, "What's up, Baby Lamuth?" I rolled my eyes at the name. My birth order in our small, tight night family mixed with our surname had been my nickname for years.

"Not much. Just sitting here," I lied.

His small eyes were intense. They had a way of looking into my soul as if reading a secret big brother code, making me feel vulnerable and exposed.

"Doesn't look like you're 'fine.' I'd say lost or even empty sounds more appropriate."

Tears stung further as I diverted my gaze, fighting them back. I wanted to lie, put on my biggest smile, and say everything was fine. But I couldn't. He would see through my dishonesty, so I settled instead on the playful banter we usually shared.

"Well, I wouldn't say I'm 'empty.' The only thing empty around here seems to be the back of your head." I forced out a quick laugh hoping it sounded genuine. But the truth was, he was right. I was empty—and lost.

"Nice try, little sis. You can attempt to deflect the conversation, but I can tell there's something wrong. You haven't been the same since Mom died. I can't say that I blame you. Her death changed all of us. But sometimes it feels like when she died, the life in your eyes did too." He didn't move. He just stared into me, waiting for me to respond. A pain stung my chest as years of his thoughts unleashed in one sentence.

My tears welled, further blurring my vision. Through the mist, I caught my aunt, who'd become our surrogate mother figure, glance in our direction. She flashed me a sympathetic smile before returning her attention to the discussion in the kitchen.

What could I say? When Mom died, a part of me died with her. I believed in God, but lately, it seemed I couldn't find Him anywhere. I certainly couldn't understand why he continued to place so much hurt and heartbreak in my life. Maybe I was strong-willed, but I was reaching the end of my limit. I felt like I was standing on the edge of a cliff, and one stiff wind was the only push I needed to jump. Lowering my eyes, I fidgeted with Sophia's teal stuffed elephant.

"I don't know what to say." Trying to release the sadness, I cleared my throat, but it didn't help. The same confusion and desperation I fought daily swelled within me.

Placing his long arm around my shoulders, Shane squeezed me into him. It felt awkward yet comforting. I barely saw him, except for these yearly Christmas visits. Yet there was something about our bond that always surprised me.

"How about you say what's on your mind, and I'll just listen?"

A few of my tears spilled over, grazing my cheek. I was powerless to stop them. But I refused to break down. Not here.

"Like I said, I don't really know what to say. Maybe I am empty. When Mom died, my whole world changed. It's like I'm not the same person. I was two halves of a whole, and life kept happening. Big, painful stuff, and I don't know how to live anymore." I paused, knowing if I continued, my composure would crumble.

"So many of my hopes and dreams for the future involved her. I know I have Joe, you, and the rest of the family, but it isn't the same. Nothing's the same." My head dropped further into his shoulder. I was ashamed of my weakness and afraid to show my vulnerability. I didn't want to care anymore.

"It's normal for you to feel this way," his hushed voice soothed my aching heart. "You and Mom were so close. Her mini-me, even. For years you were like two peas in a pod." He wiped at a tear on my cheek. "Even though she's gone, one thing you'll always have are the memories, and those are powerful. I operate under a persistent philosophy in life. When I'm sad, I reflect on what I have more than what I don't."

"Mom lived long enough to be well-remembered by key people, us kids for example, and that lives beyond her. So while our littles may not have that, they will always have our memories of her, in her absence. There is always something we have that can help overshadow the sadness of what we are missing. You have such a strong faith, something I've never fully shared with you. But I'm confident that your faith would tell you her spirit's still here with you. When she exists in your memory, she can also exist in your future."

His words struck my heart like lightning to my soul. Lifting my head from his shoulder, I stared at him as if my entire life were unfolding from a new perspective. *When she exists in your memory, she can also exist in your future.* "That's it! That's what I've been missing all this time. I can still take her on every trip we dreamed of and teach the girls about her—they can know her and love her. This changes everything."

Air filled my lungs to a capacity I hadn't felt in years. I remembered everything about her, from the way her eyes twinkled when she smiled to the way her bottom lip quivered when she tried to fight off tears. There was the soft, almost muffled sound her voice made when she was being serious, or the way we had entire conversations no one else could understand. Every last part of her still existed in my memory. In awe of his words, I studied my brother. Though I knew Shane didn't fully believe in God the way I did, there was no doubt God was behind this.

"My goodness, Shane. You are so right. I've been wrapped in my shell of grief for so long that I neglected to realize, as long as I'm alive, in a way, so is she." I shook him slightly. "Don't you see? This changes everything!"

No longer did the world around me dull into the background. Rather, it exploded with new vibrancy. "I've missed you."

Throwing my arms around his neck, I hugged him tightly, kissing his scruffy cheek, and rubbed a hand on his thinning hair.

"Looks like age has made you wise, old man." I laughed, full and free.

"You liked that, huh? I call that scripture from the mind of Shane. Then again, I'm an introspective guy with a degree in psychology, so I think differently." We both laughed. His smile brought back the wrinkles near his eyes.

Wrapping my arms once more around his strong shoulders, I whispered, "You may think that's 'scripture from the mind of Shane,' but I know better. I know *exactly* where those words came from." My eyes glanced heavenward. "And I know exactly what to do with them. I'll rewrite my story."

A LETTER TO MY MOTHER

I see your name etched into stone. The finality of your birth and death is carved for all eternity. You've been gone more than ten years, but I still remember you like no time has passed. Nearly a decade has eased my pain and grief, but it can never eliminate the emptiness. There's a hollow feeling in the middle of my chest that aches when I remember you are gone. I know it's okay because the death of someone you loved is not something you get over. It is something you survive.

You nurtured me into the sassy, smart, caring, grateful person I am. As my mother, your life created me, and that realization will remain forever. Your life taught me a faith strong enough to triumph over death and beautiful, whole, unconditional love. No person could love me the way you did. No one.

The way you lived taught me fortitude, even in the midst of the vast hardship of disease. I would have given up. But not you. You fought.

Your living taught me joy—full-out, unstoppable, and pure—the joy of loving with eloquent simplicity.

But your death, in stark contrast, created a vast wound that irrevocably changed the landscape of my soul. Over time, the wound has begun to heal—in its place, a scar I wear as a badge of honor in remembrance. My precious memories of you live in me, so deeply etched even the winds and sands of time could never erode them.

Well-meaning people, therapists, and friends have told me that grief is a process I must go through. And I agree. Your death is something I'm still processing.

Grief hurts—to the bones, filtering through the marrow kind of pain. It weaved its way into my being, taking up residency. They say grief comes in stages. I've seen them all.

The denial was powerful and even surprising, given your death was prolonged by your disease. Years later, I'm still struck by the pang of truth you're no longer here.

Anger came quickly, expected, given how tightly you were woven into the fabric of my life. I still feel the flames of anger linger in my heart. But my anger comforted me in your absence. It shielded me from the attempts of others to console me. It was my barrier to the rest of the world. I isolated myself from everyone and any unnecessary activity. Blocking all emotion for fear of losing any remaining strength I had, I forced myself into autopilot. Each day was a haze of necessary obligations nestled between the safety of seclusion. Without you, life seemed devoid of the joy and love you radiated. When my anger grew especially strong, I could hear your gentle voice reminding me, "Let go, Sunshine. Don't be angry too long. God didn't take me to hurt you but to save me. Wrap yourself in His love, because my love is there too."

The sadness I contained blurred the reality of life. I was a foreigner in my own skin, lost in an unknown landscape. Searching for help, I cried out to God. I broke down my wall of anger, and in its place, I offered Him my outstretched hand and tear-stained cheeks. Reaching up to my Creator, I knew only He could calm this storm raging within. So much hurt tore me apart until I finally realized the One who could heal all the brokenness.

God waited for my return. In hindsight, I can see it was Him who helped me find each piece of myself, and with painstaking precision, guided me to put them back together. Though it would be months before we could speak again, I know He was always there holding the broken pieces together. I realized, through Him, I could find my joy again.

Faith was the most important virtue you taught me in your living. Your faith from a hospital bed enlightened more people to the beauty of God than even the best-delivered sermon. To have faith in myself, in the goodness of others, and most importantly, in God was the secret to surviving my grief. So, I vowed that day to take the open hand of God and allow Him to lift me up off the ground.

I vowed to honor you, Mom, every day of my life. I vowed to let God calm my storms while I praised Him in the patient surrender of my suffering.

With the gradual passage of time, God has brought healing to my pain. Though your death still stings, I will take the hurt and heartache, for they are evidence that you lived. You touched the souls of everyone who met you. Your radiant smile and childlike love of life blessed us all. I promised you, your presence would live forever in the memories of those who loved you, and I have kept true to my word. Your spirit comes wherever I go. Every adventure I take that you couldn't, the sound of your laughter still echoes in my ear. I saw your face, eyes wide with childlike excitement experiencing Disneyworld, the ocean, and in every adventure, you joined me in spirit.

I've told my children about you. They know how much you loved them, even though you've never met them.

The other night as I put Lillian to bed, she was hugging the pillow you made for her before you passed. She searched for the smudgy inked fingerprint in the folds of the fabric. Looking up at me with her sad, tired eyes, she whispered, "Mommy, I miss Grandma Vicki. I love her so much." In that instant, joy encompassed me because I knew, even though you're gone, my memories keep you alive in their hearts, too.

I've told people of the beauty you placed in this world while you were here. We remember you on holidays and special family occasions. We speak "Vicklish" and share memories of you until our stomachs hurt from laughter. I've continued to fight the disease that stole your life, and I promise to continue as long as I live.

You, too, have kept your word. You've sent me the butterflies you promised on every trip I've taken. I saw them fluttering outside the window of the hospital when both my girls were born, and on every one of "our trips" we were going to take. Sometimes, they appear just when I need a reminder you're always with me. I feel your presence when they are near. They've landed on my hand, on my head, and in my heart.

Mom, I promise to share our story, one of love and redemption over death. I promise to encourage those who have lost someone they love to keep that love alive in every moment of life, letting them know that even though death may have taken their loved one, they never have to live without them. As long as I'm living, your legacy will, too.

Until the day we meet again, save a place for me. Well done good and faithful servant, well done.

Love Always,

Sunshine

AUTHOR'S NOTE

Dear Reader,

Every life contains a story. A combined sum of circumstances and events written into our lives by one benevolent author, God. My story, like yours, holds tragic, soul-defining chapters I deemed unfair. But fairness is not the rulebook for the Author of Life—it is reckless, all-consuming love.

When we look at every situation through the lens of this unending love and desire for our betterment, we begin to embrace even the most difficult details as opportunities for growth. This new view can illuminate a calling or purpose for our lives which may otherwise remain locked in the darkness of despair.

I pray you might make the choice, as I have, to look at the most challenging chapters of your life with new eyes. Don't remain locked in heartache or grief. Take a step today to move beyond suffering into joy. Today is the day you rewrite your story.

In this together,
Sonya Joy Mack

PHOTO GALLERY

Sonya's early years—
fourth-grade greatness, 1990

Sonya and Vicki on Vicki's first
trip to the ocean, 2006

"Two Peas in a God-pod," 2008

Vicki at her first Walk to Defeat ALS, 2009

Vicki praying over quilts she helped "make" at the sweatshop, 2009

Sophia's newborn photos at six weeks, following major surgery to remove a portion of her right lung, 2016

Sonya, Lillian, and Sophia visiting Grandma Vicki's gravesite, 2020

The House of Mack: Joe, Sonya, Lillian, and Sophia, 2020

ABOUT THE AUTHOR

Sonya Joy Mack has treated grief and illness for over fifteen years as a physician assistant in family medicine and plastic and reconstructive surgery. In the grief of her mother's passing, Sonya became ignited with a passion to bring joy and purpose to women everywhere. She created The LIVE JOY LIFE, an organization that empowers women through community, mindset, and the LIVE JOY principles, to live in the joy God intended. Her work has appeared in the Guideposts compilation, *In the Arms of Angels*, as a guest blogger for "The Well Des Moines," and on her personal author page. Sonya lives in Des Moines, Iowa with her husband and two spunky daughters, where she enjoys red wine, dark chocolate, big hugs, and living room dance parties. Sonya continues to advocate for a treatment and cure for ALS, the disease that took her mother's life.

Sonya would like to invite you to join her on Instagram @sonyajoymack, Facebook at www.facebook.com/SonyaJoyMackAuthor, or become a part of the LIVE JOY LIFE family at www.sonyajoymack.com.

A free ebook edition is available with the purchase of this book.

To claim your free ebook edition:

1. Visit MorganJamesBOGO.com
2. Sign your name CLEARLY in the space
3. Complete the form and submit a photo of the entire copyright page
4. You or your friend can download the ebook to your preferred device

Morgan James
BOGO™

A **FREE** ebook edition is available for you
or a friend with the purchase of this print book.

CLEARLY SIGN YOUR NAME ABOVE

Instructions to claim your free ebook edition:
1. Visit MorganJamesBOGO.com
2. Sign your name CLEARLY in the space above
3. Complete the form and submit a photo of this entire page
4. You or your friend can download the ebook to your preferred device

Print & Digital Together Forever.

Snap a photo

Free ebook

Read anywhere

CPSIA information can be obtained
at www.ICGtesting.com
Printed in the USA
JSHW030243141122
32878JS00001BA/8